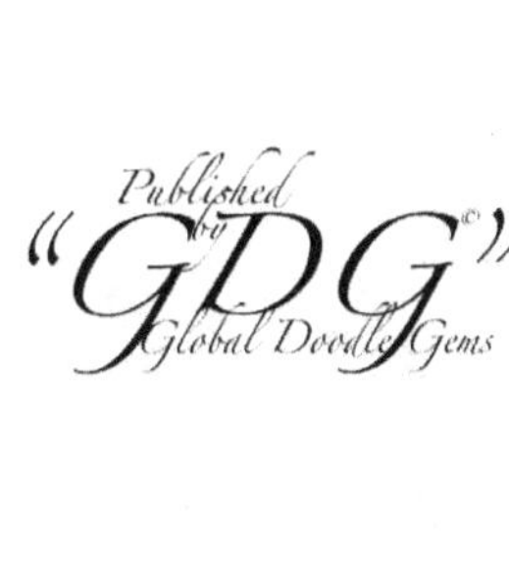

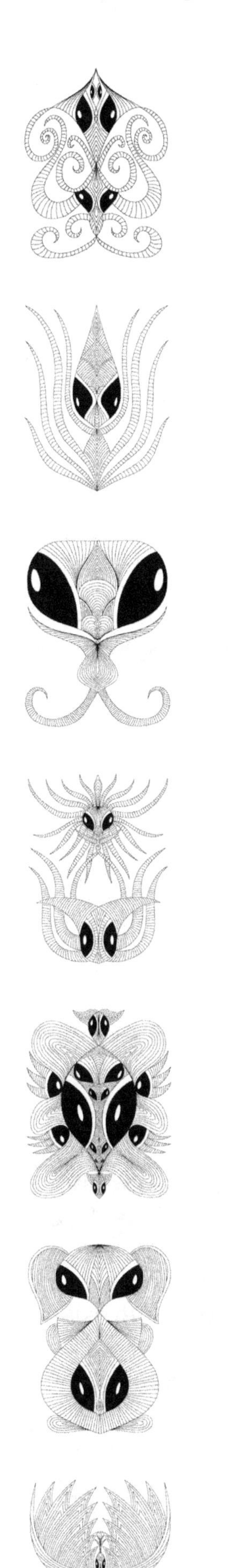
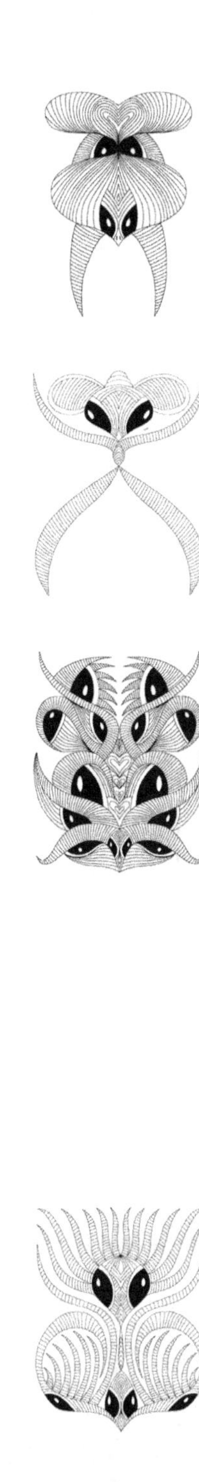
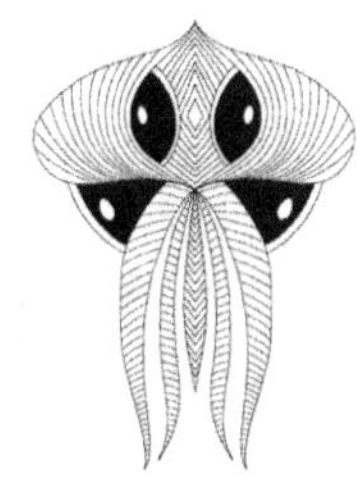

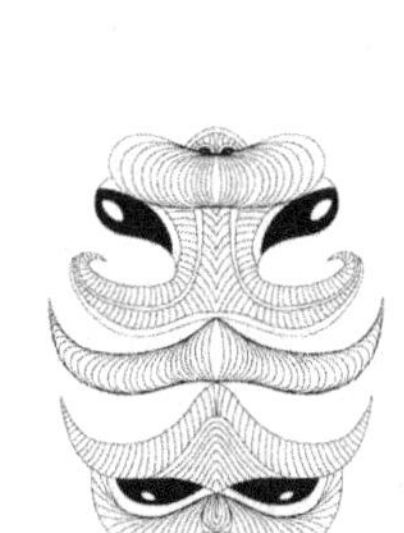
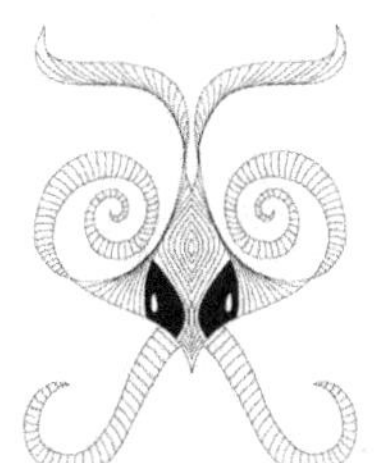
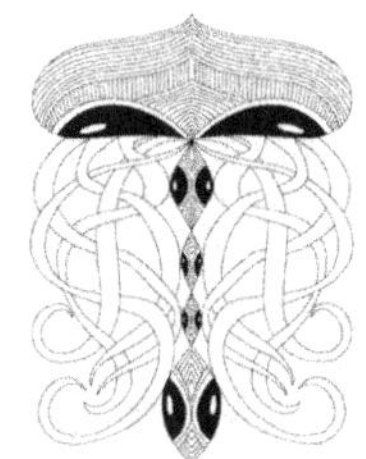
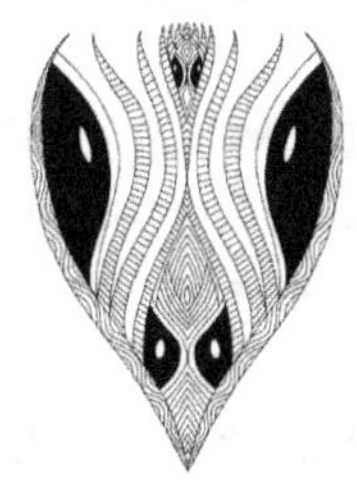
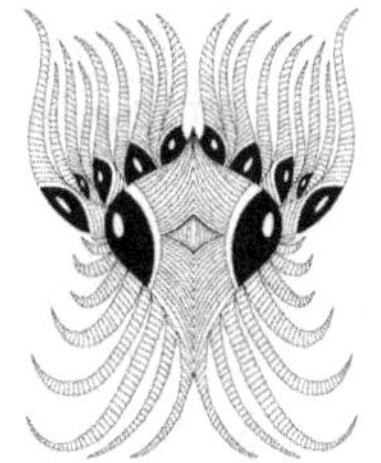
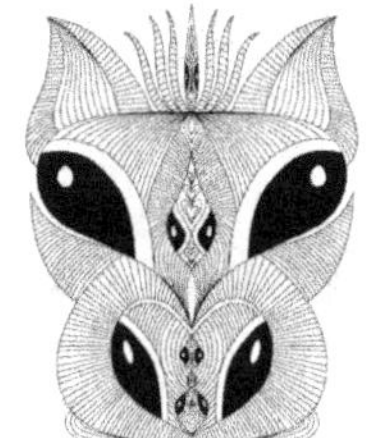
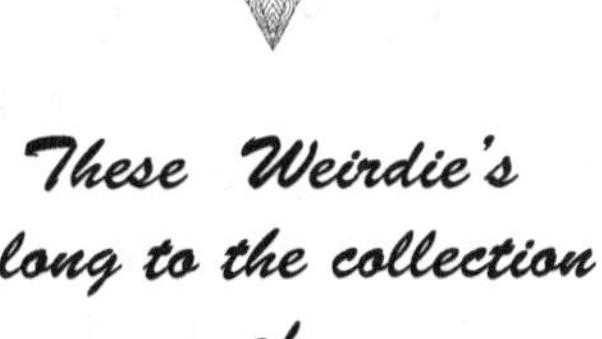

These Weirdie's
belong to the collection
of

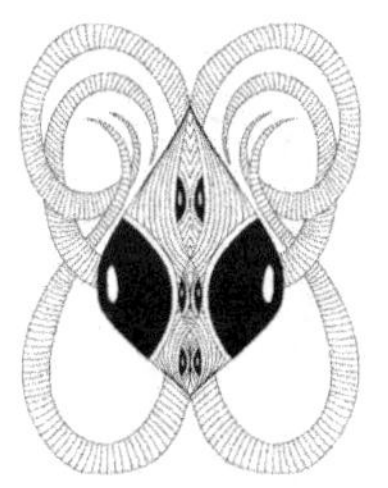
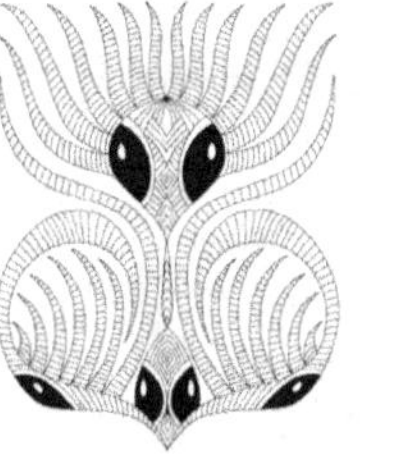
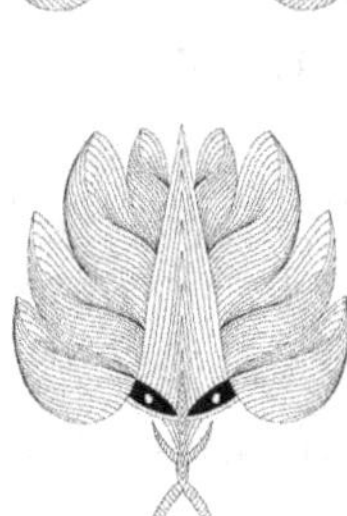
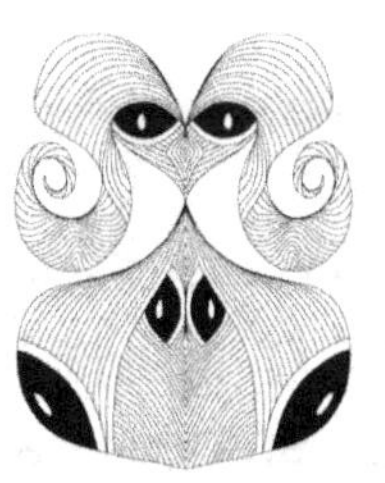
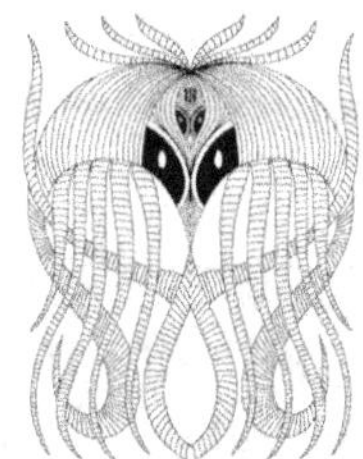
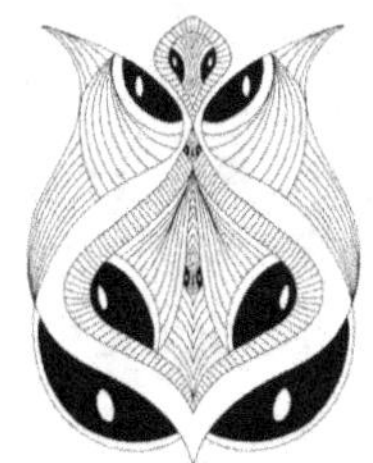
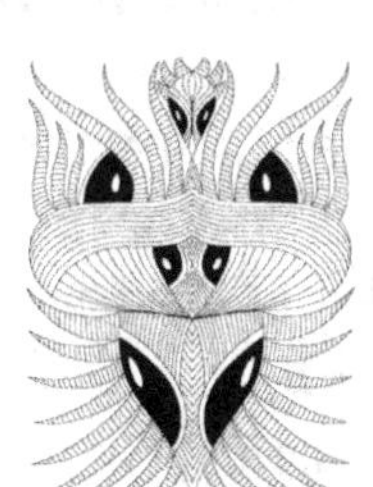
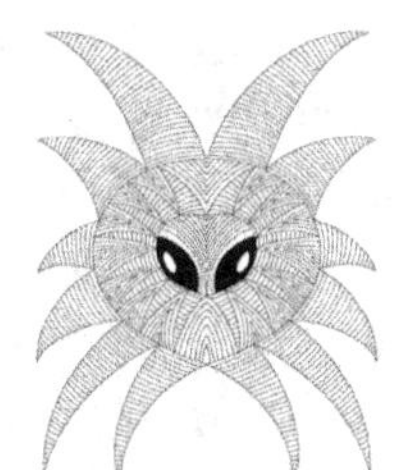
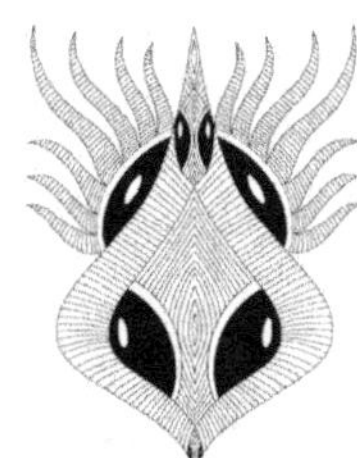
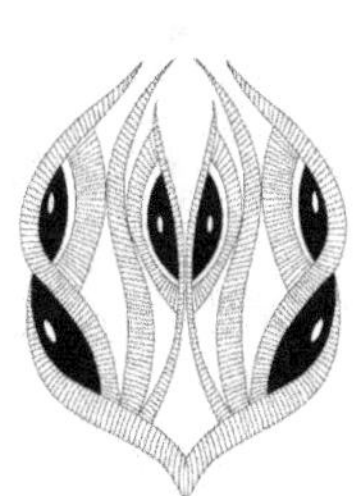
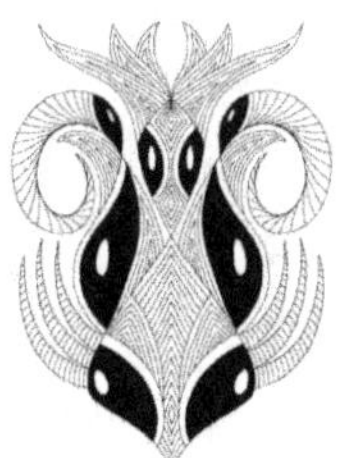
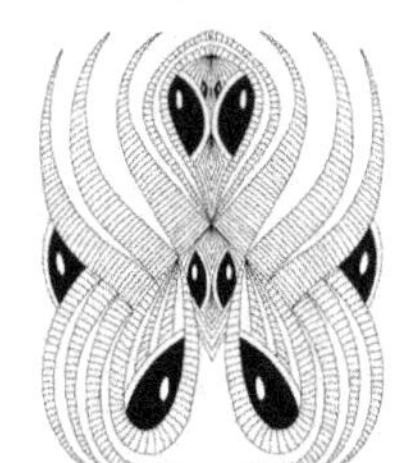

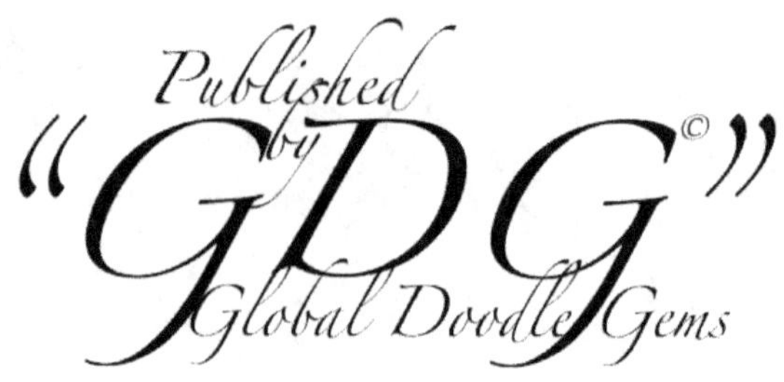

Share your colored versions with us ! We love seeing your results
and hearing from you
we are social !

The Official FB book page, stay on top of what we have in the works !
www.facebook.com/AMVWART
The Community group, share your colored pages, meet the artists, enjoy exclusive freebies, take part in community Charity books and so much more......
www.facebook.com/groups/ColorAWeirdieADay
Follow us on Twitter.... @GlobalDoodlegem
We are on Instagram too
@globaldoodlegems for instagram
...and if you are not social like that we have a blog
globaldoodlegems.wordpress.com

Welcome to my world of Weirdies

This is the seventh weirdies book of year 5 of Color A Weirdie A Day,
join us for daily coloring with either me or one of the wonderful guesthosts
at the group www.facebook.com/groups/ColorAWeirdieADay,
and check out all the beautiful colored !
The set has 12 books Weirdies 49 to Weirdies 60, one book for each month
with a Weirdie for each day, additionally all Weirdies are repeated in the
back of the book in their upside_down versions ...
Your Weirdie can drastically change and turn in to a brand new Weirdie.
Get your Weirdie on and have a fun and relaxing time with coloring it,
join the group and show your colored, join the live coloring and have fun
with us ... if you like !
Weirdies 1 to 12 were colored live in 2018 Weirdies 13 to 24 were colored live in 2019 Weirdies 25 to 36 were colored 2020 and Weirdies 37
to 48 were colored in 2021

Weirdies 49 will be colored in January 2022 Daily
Weirdies 50 will be colored in February 2022 Daily
Weirdies 51 will be colored in March 2022 Daily
Weirdies 52 will be colored in April 2022 Daily
Weirdies 53 will be colored in May 2022 Daily
Weirdies 54 will be colored in June 2022 Daily
Weirdies 55 will be colored in July 2022 Daily

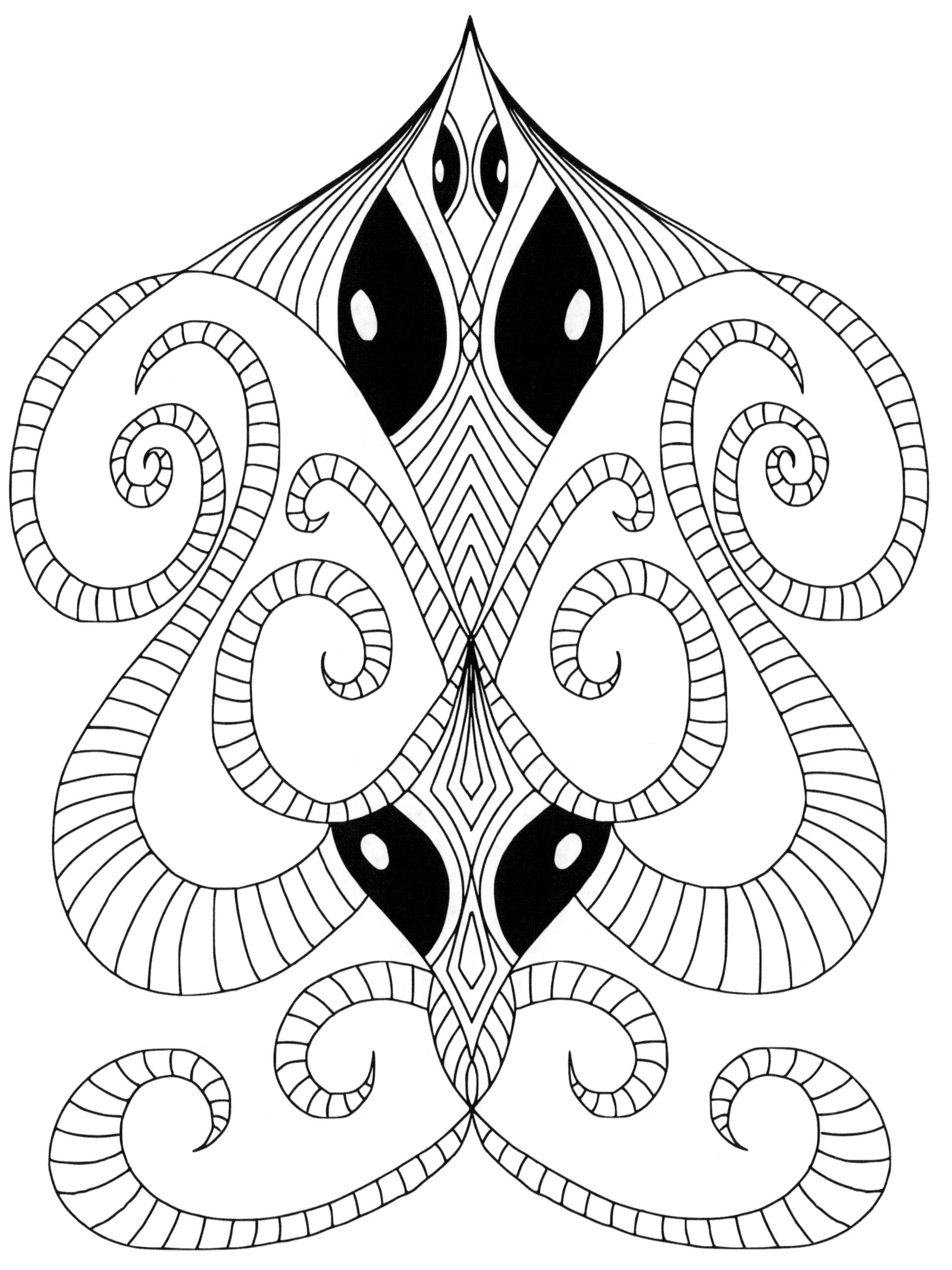

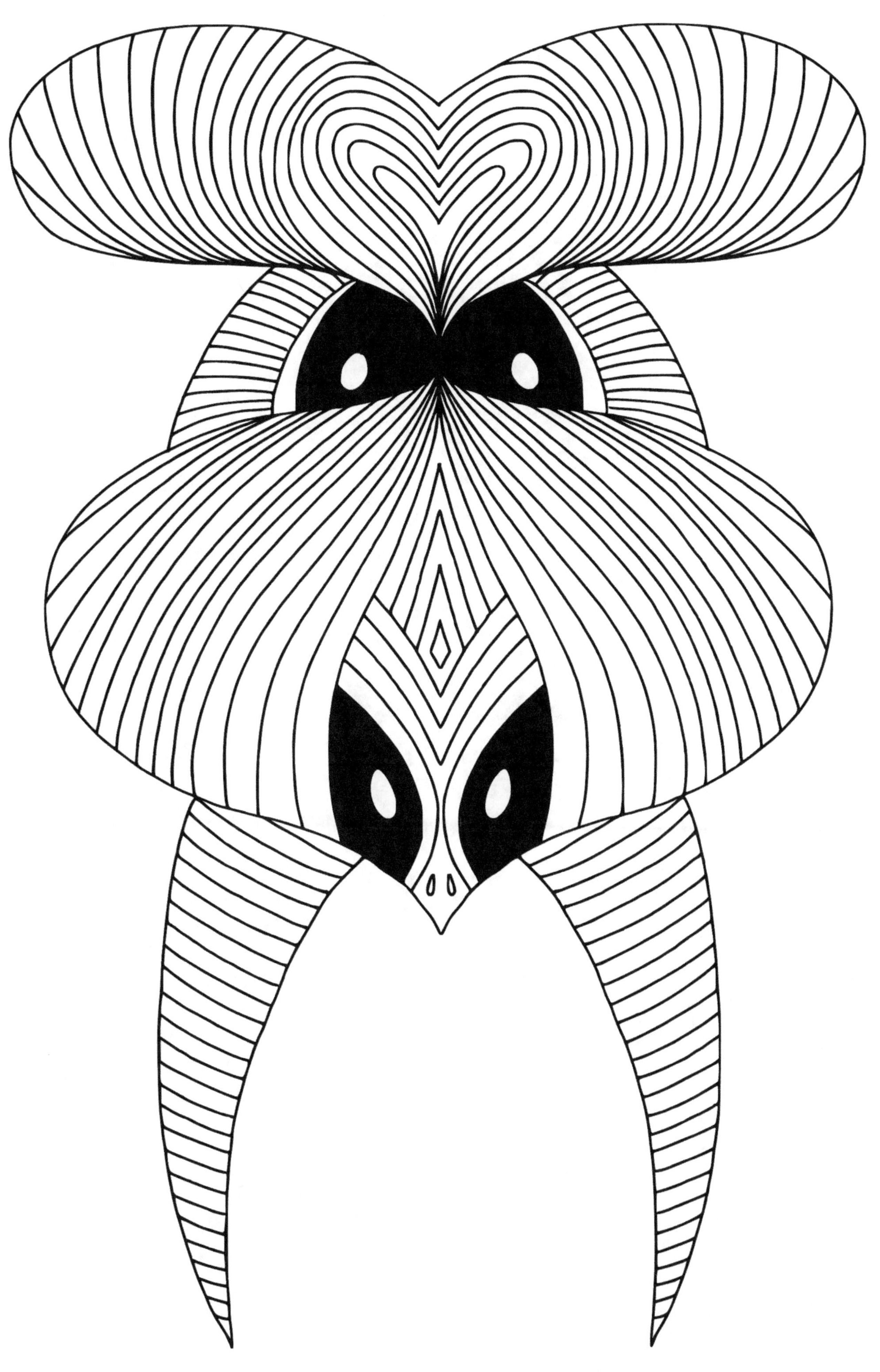

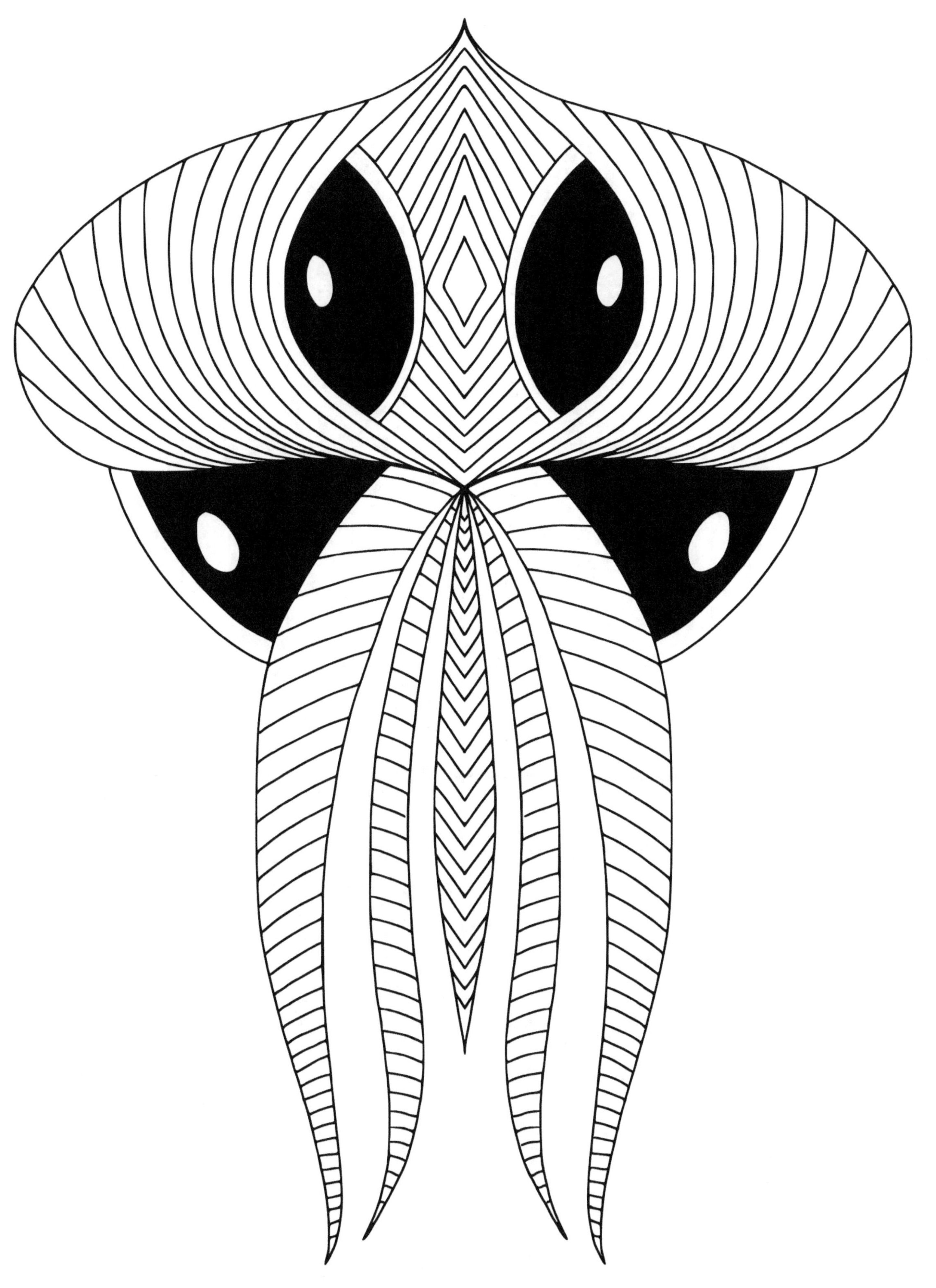

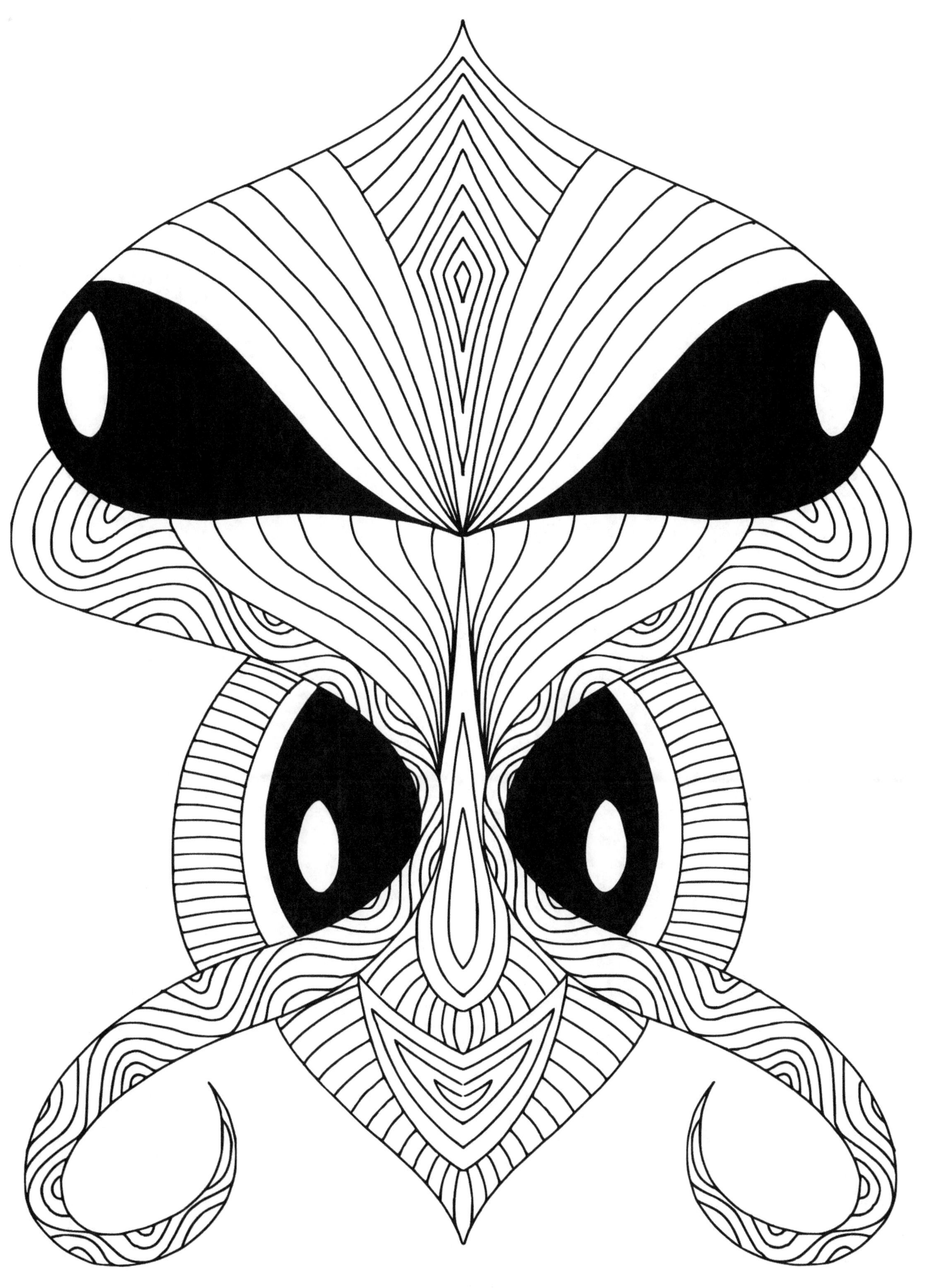

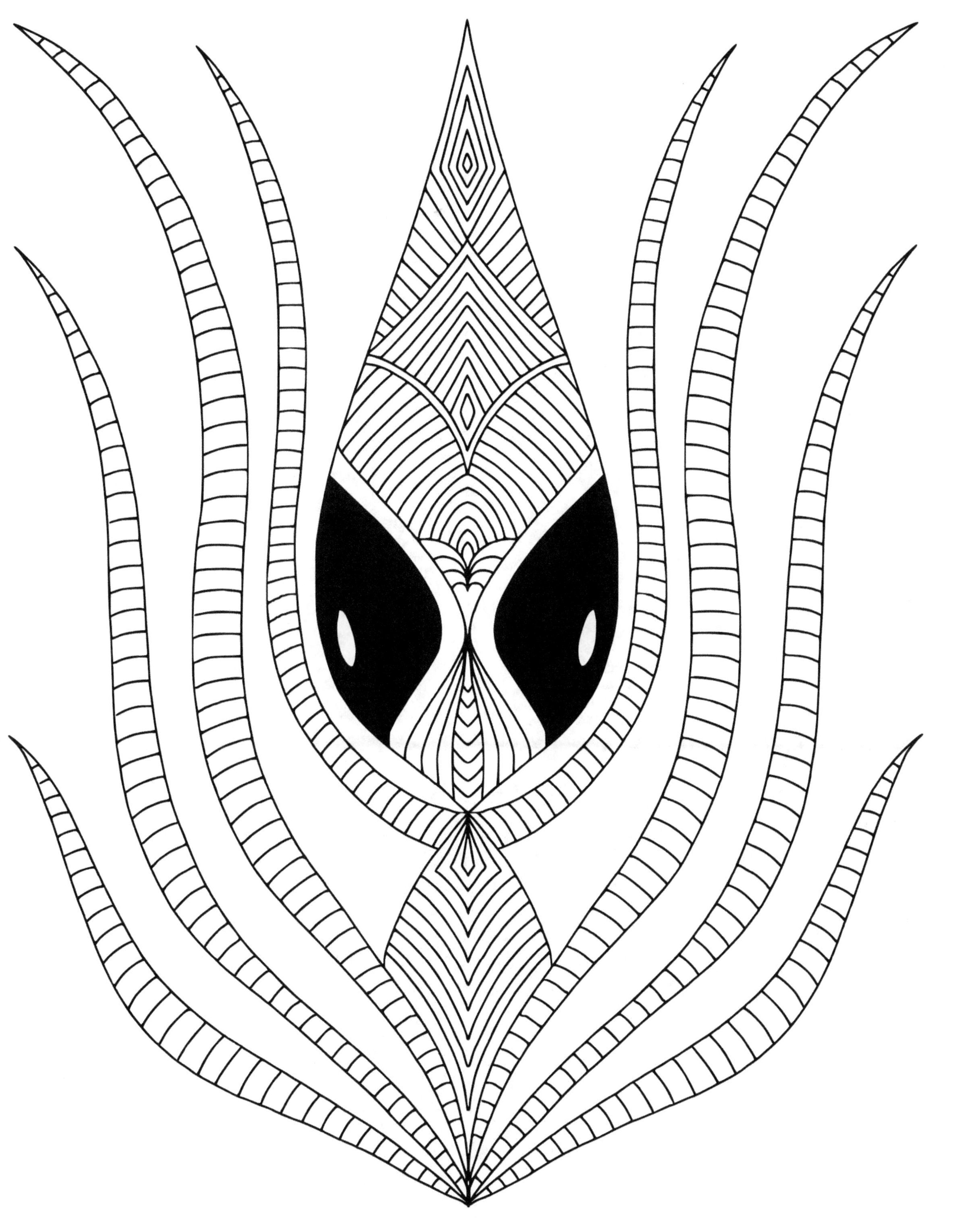

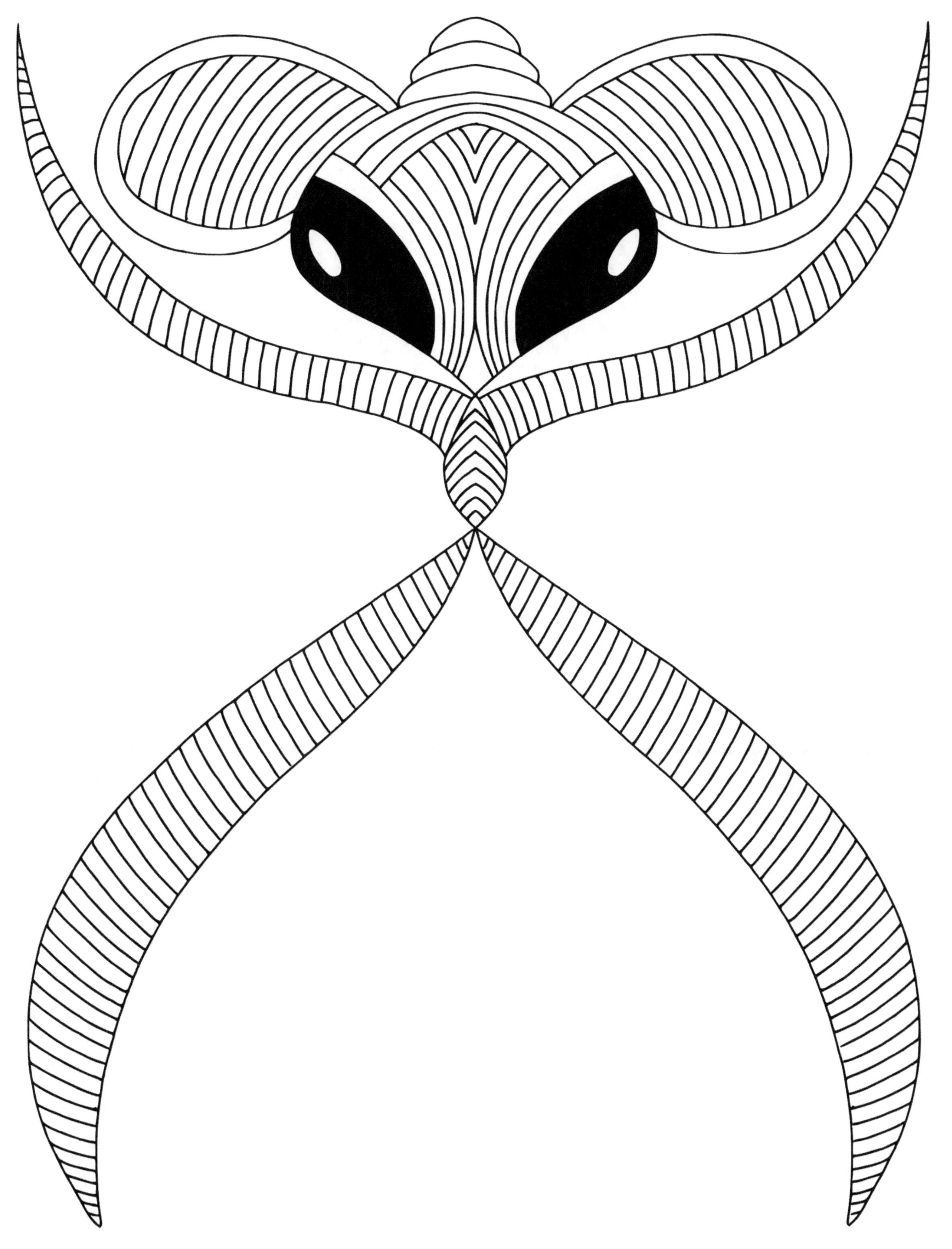

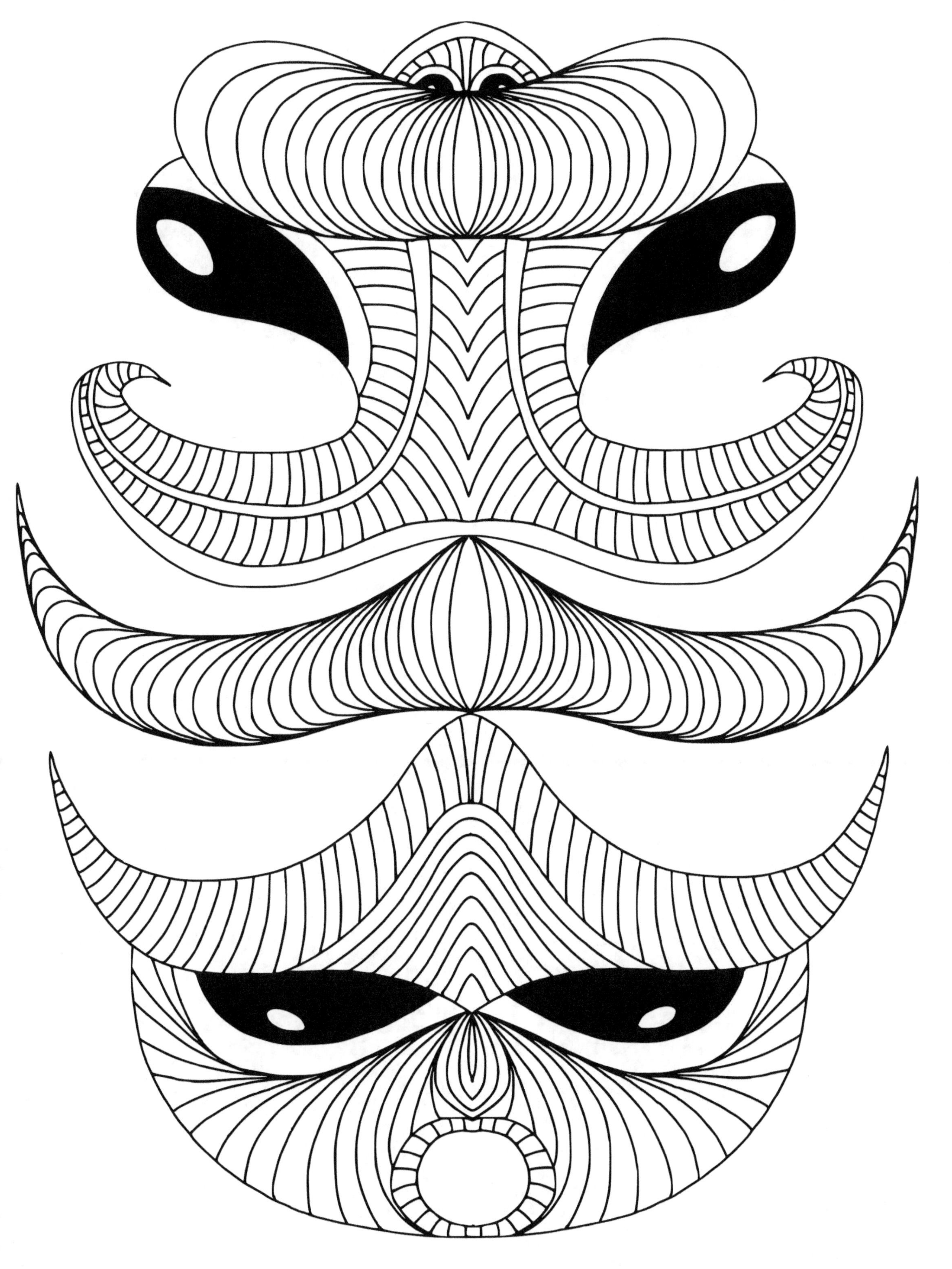

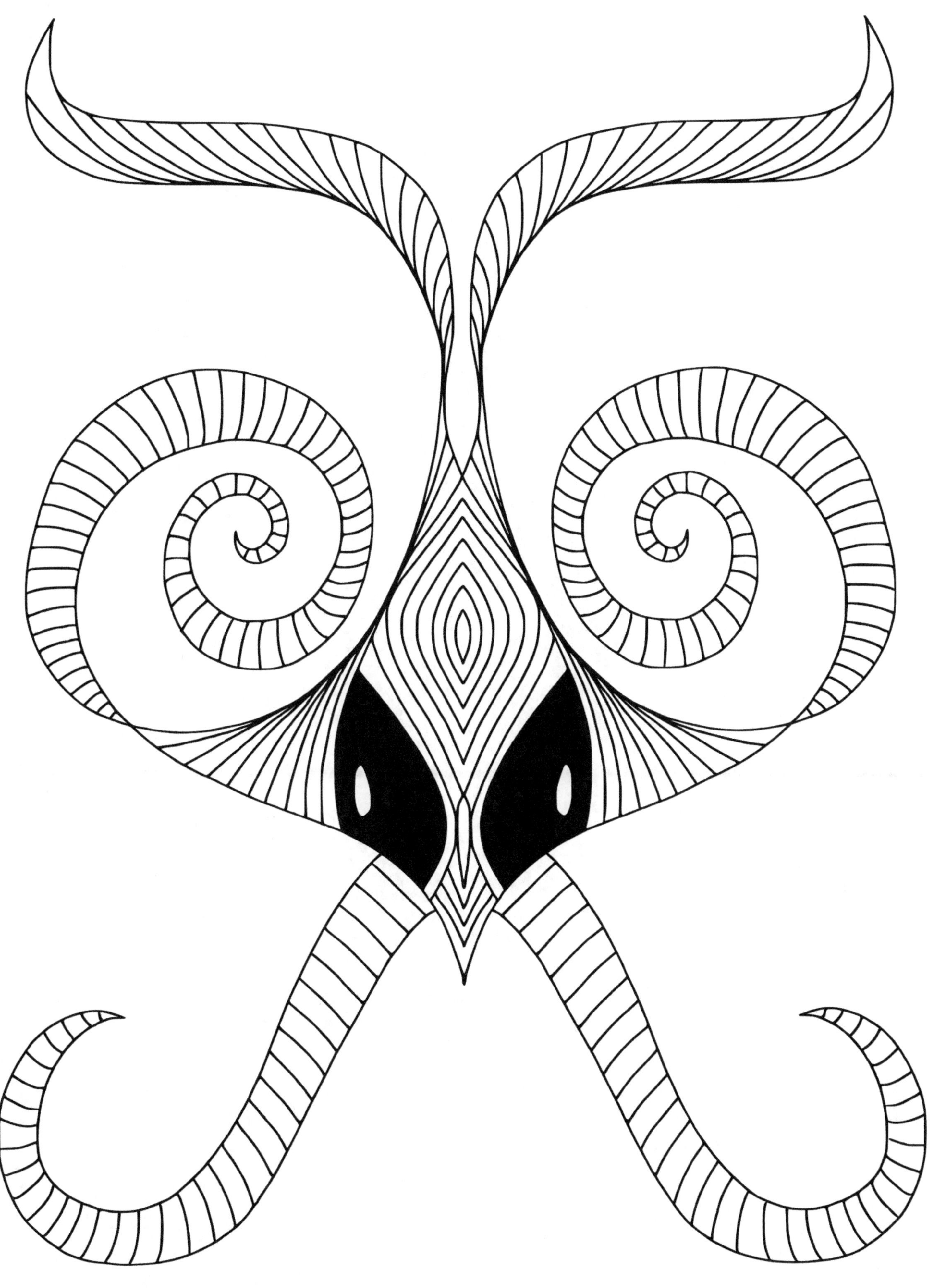

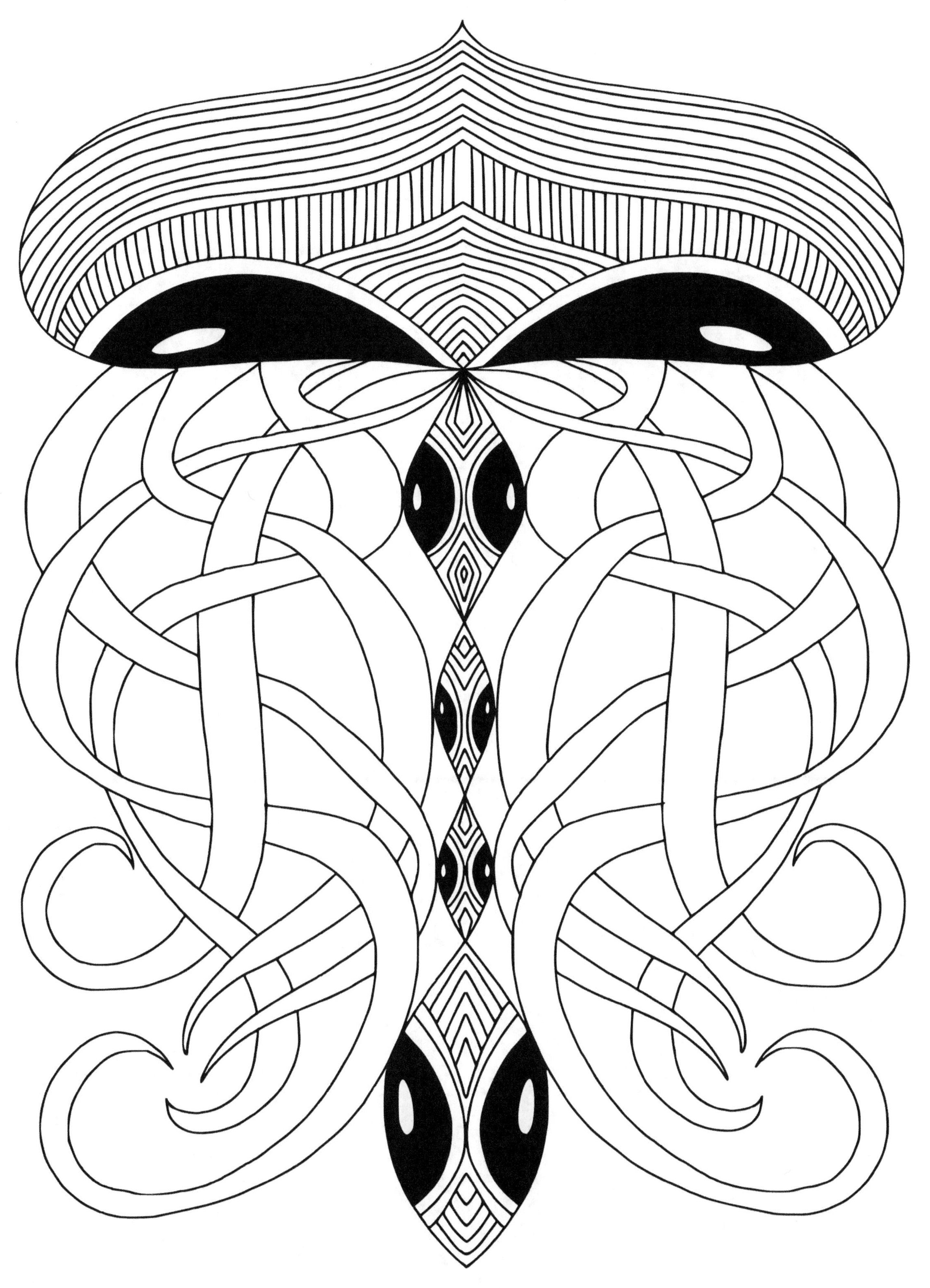

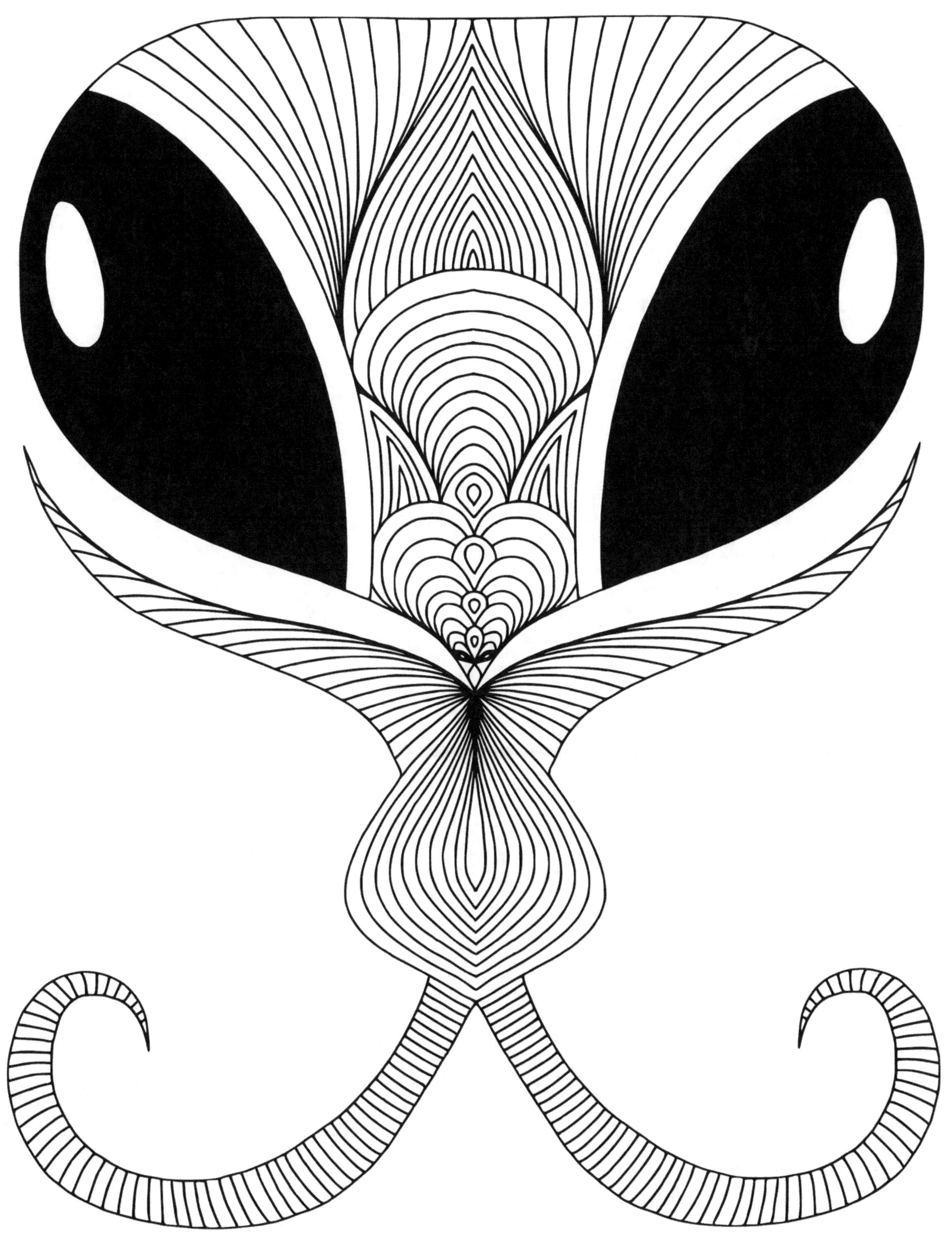

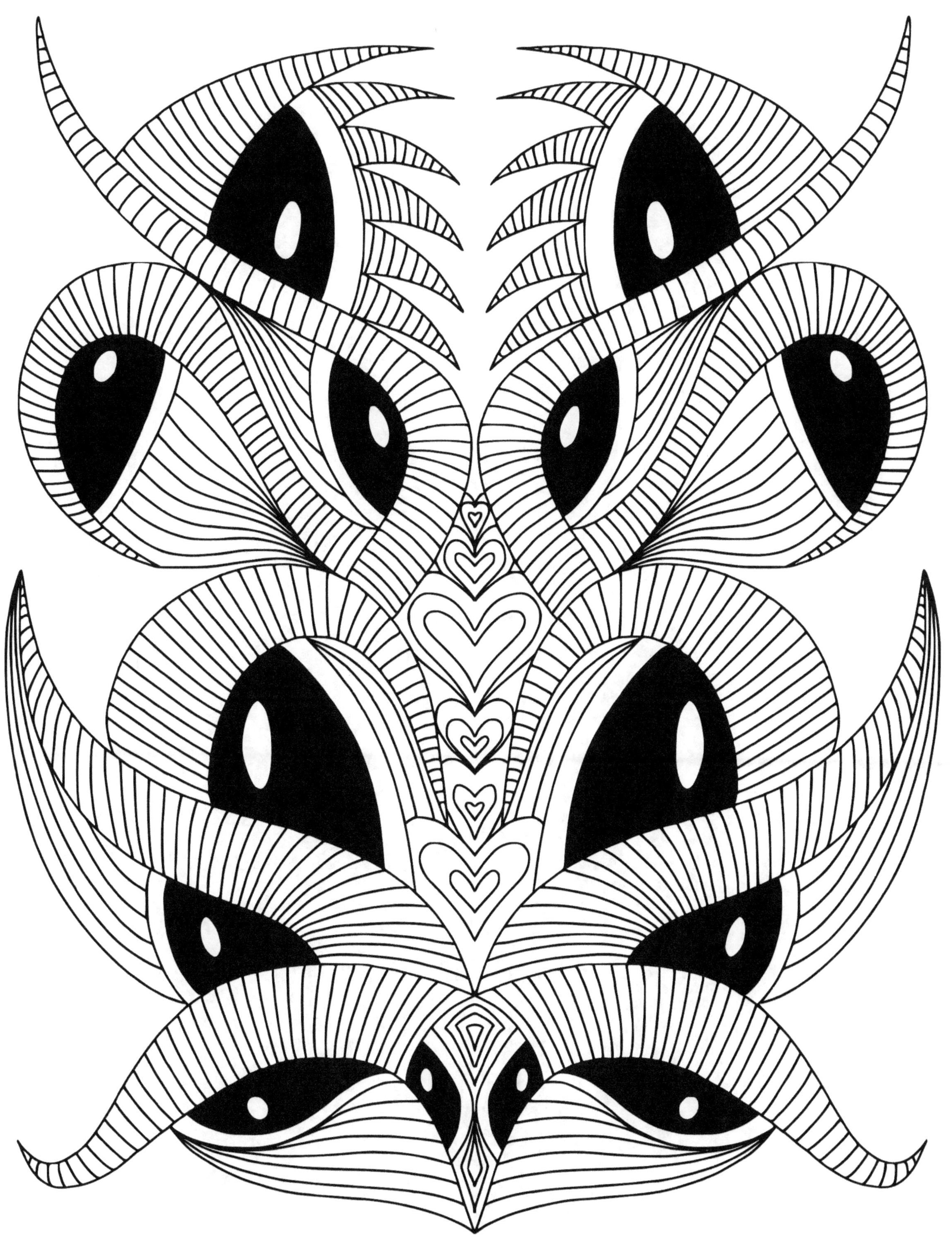

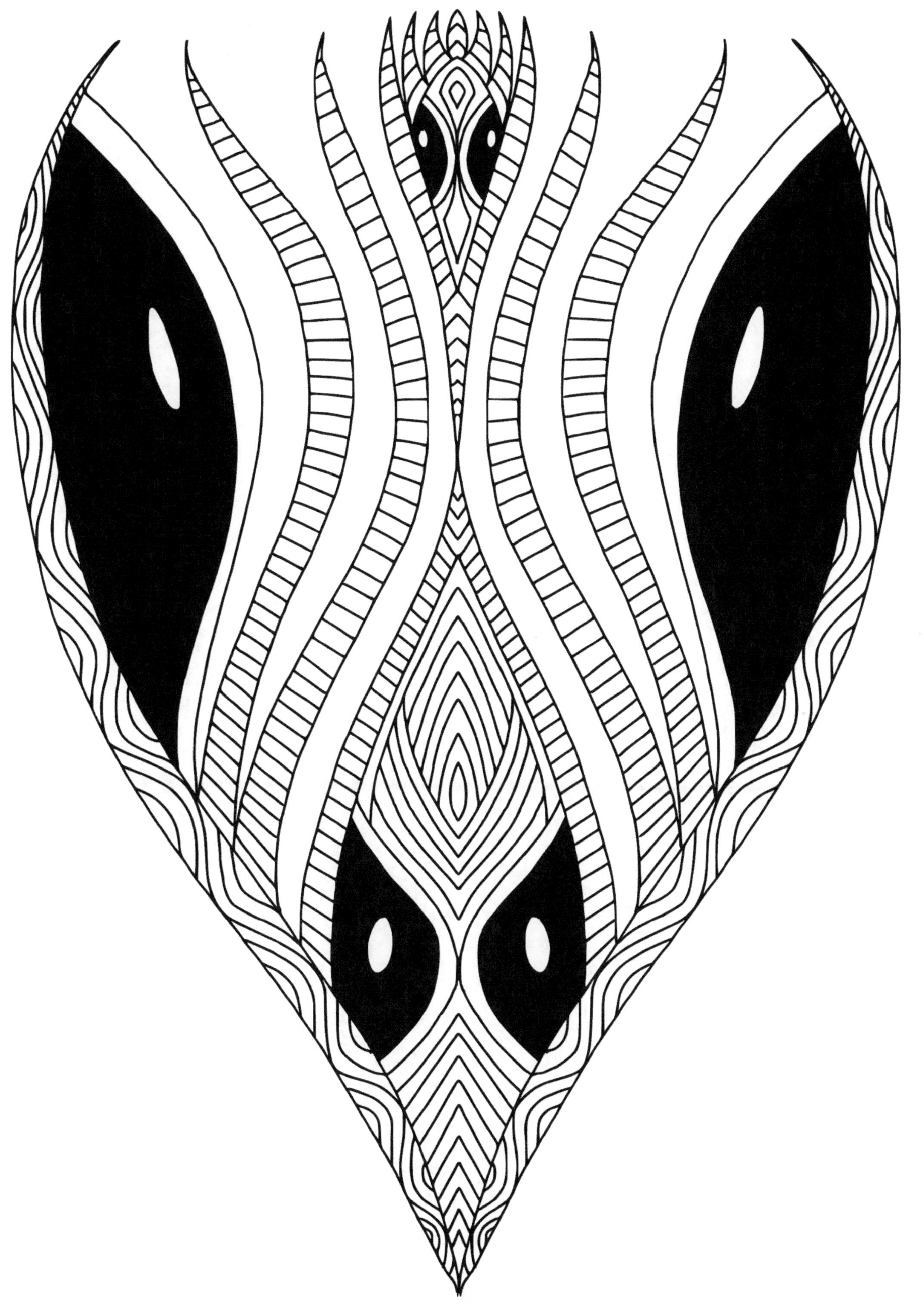

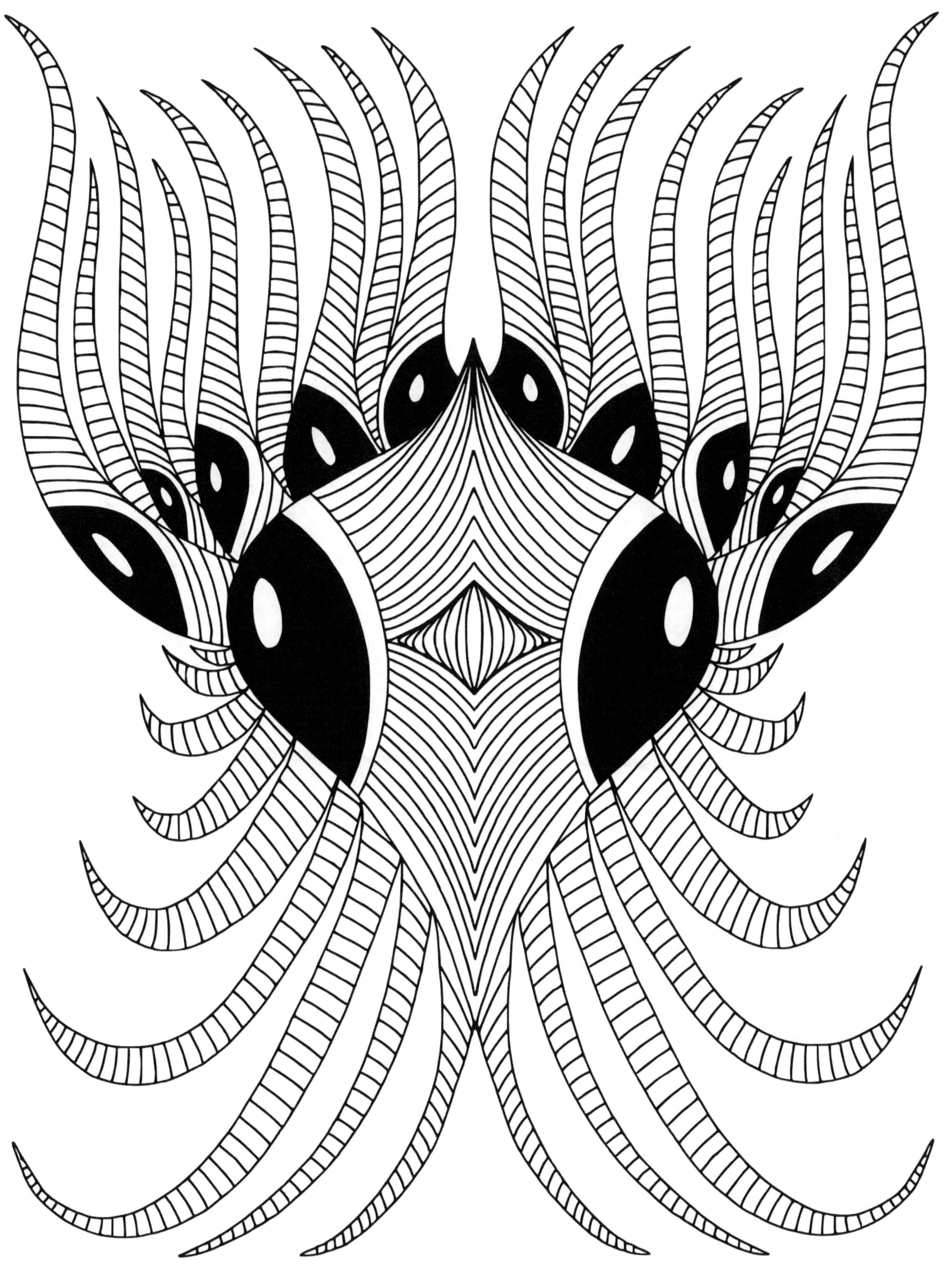

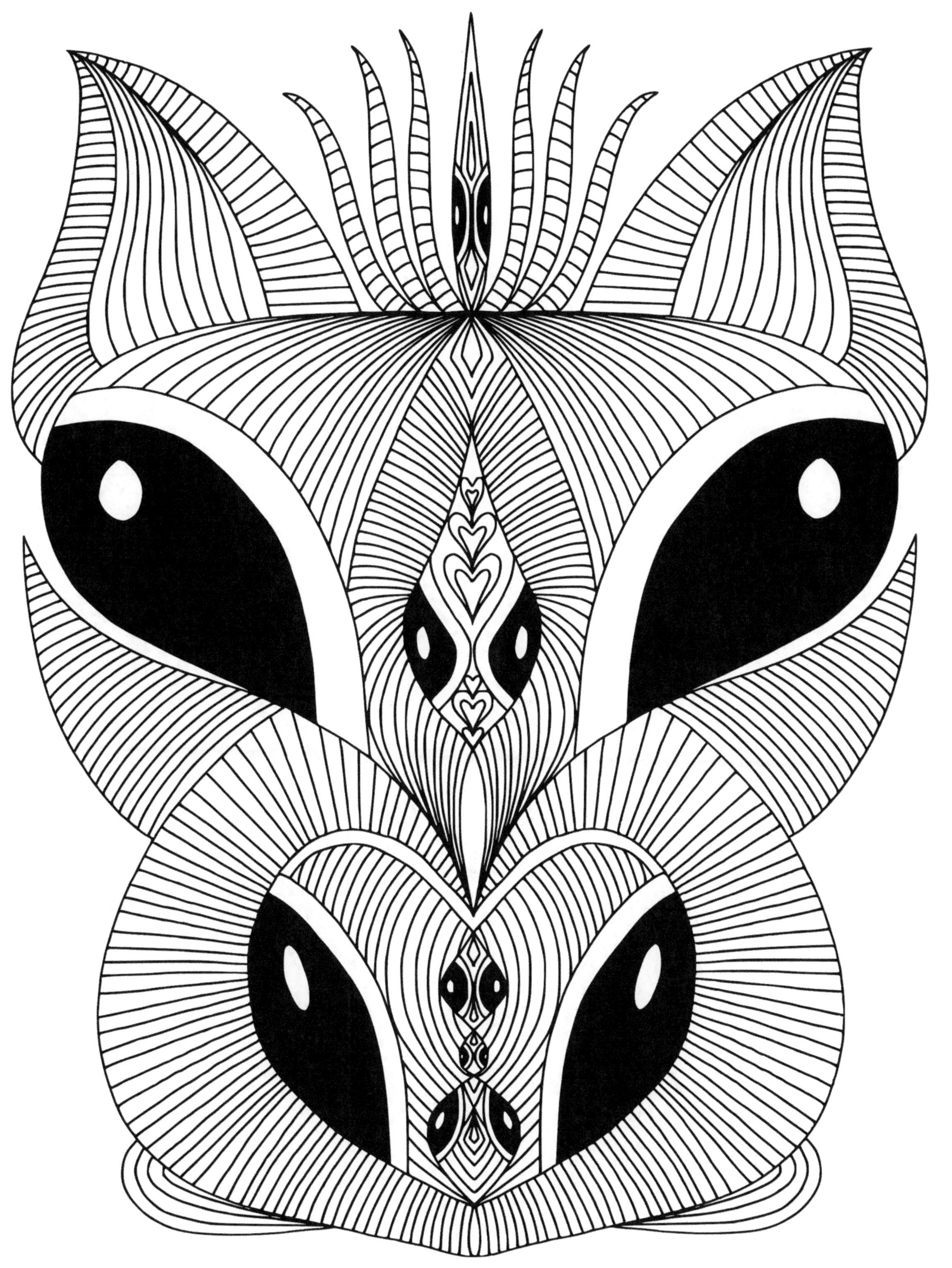

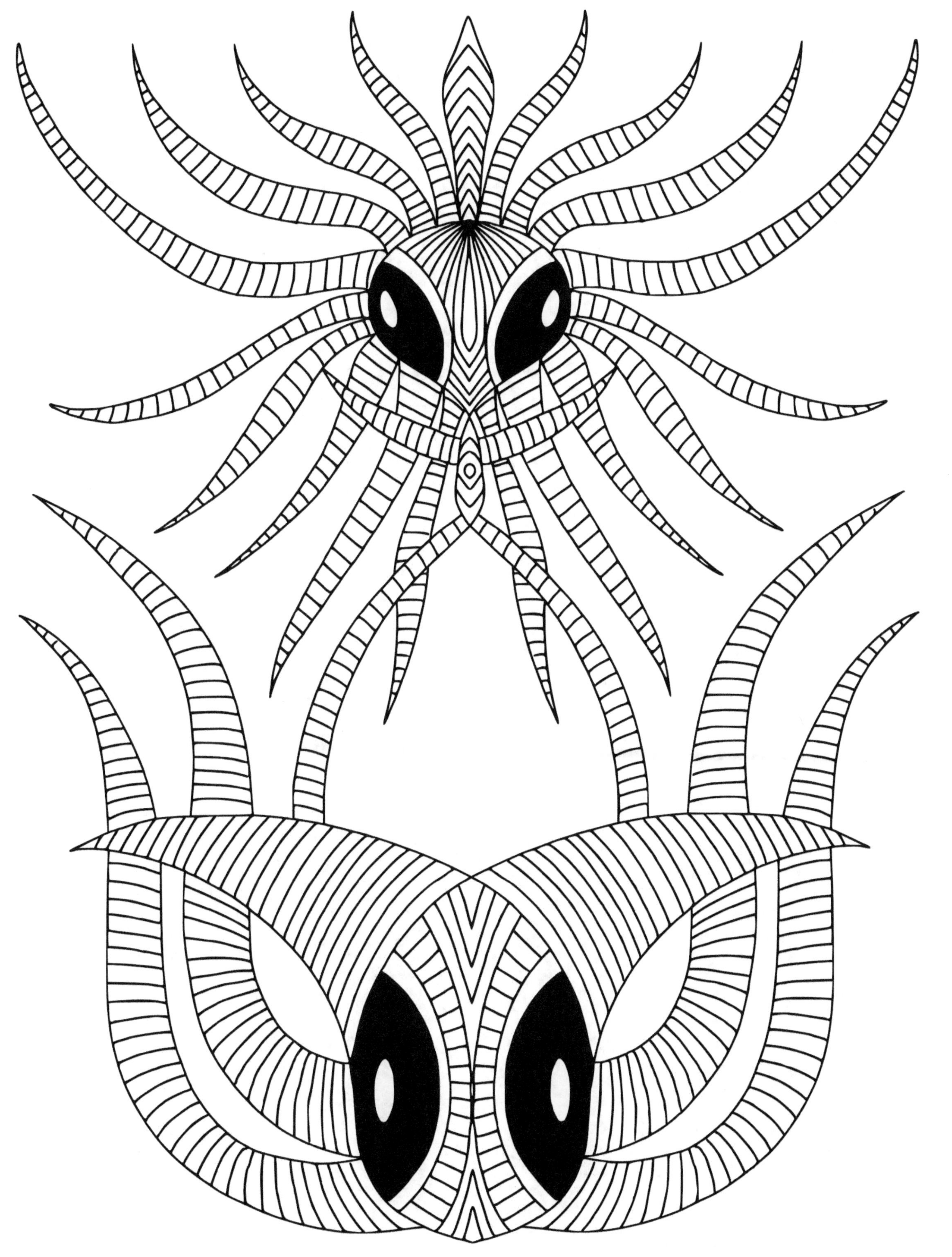

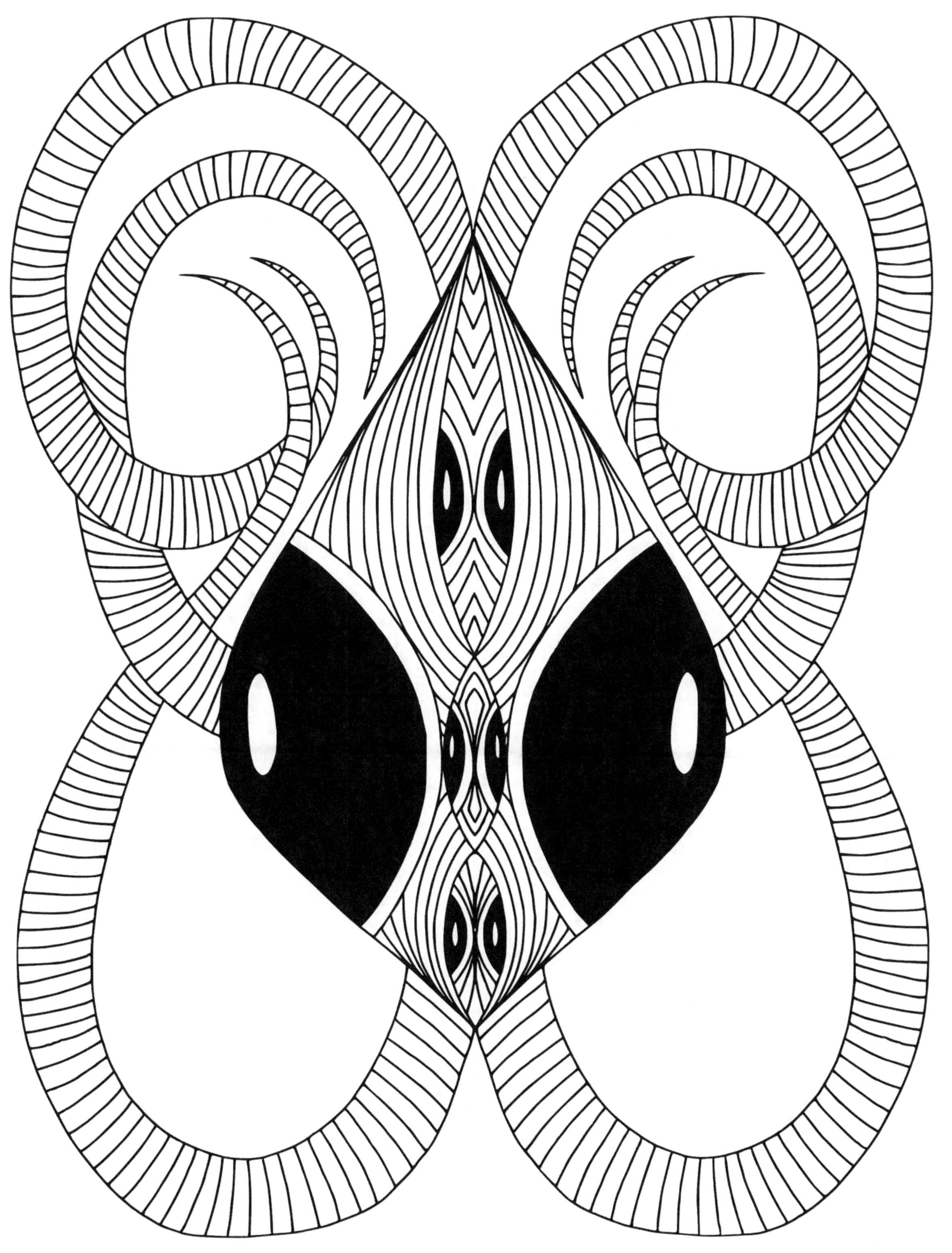

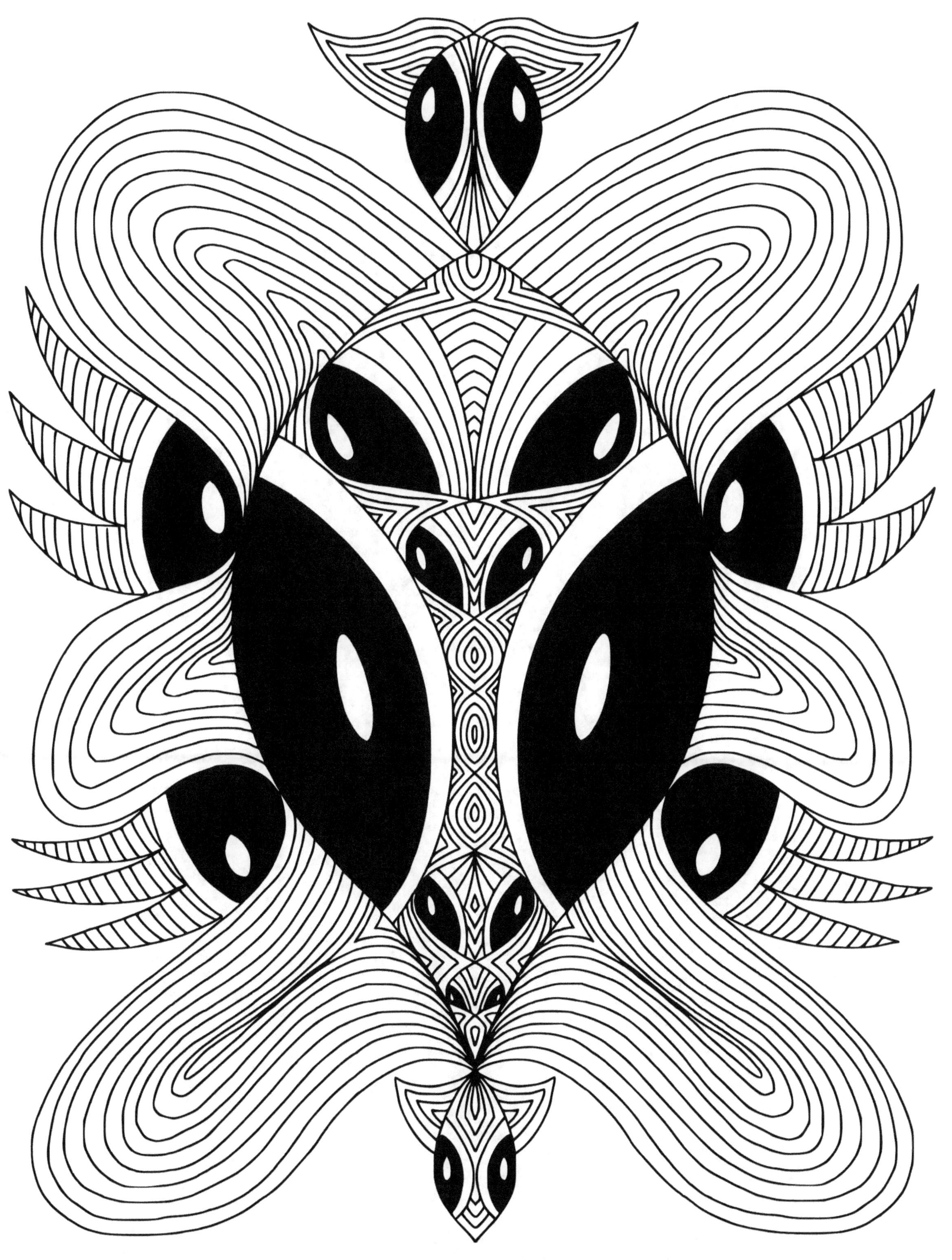

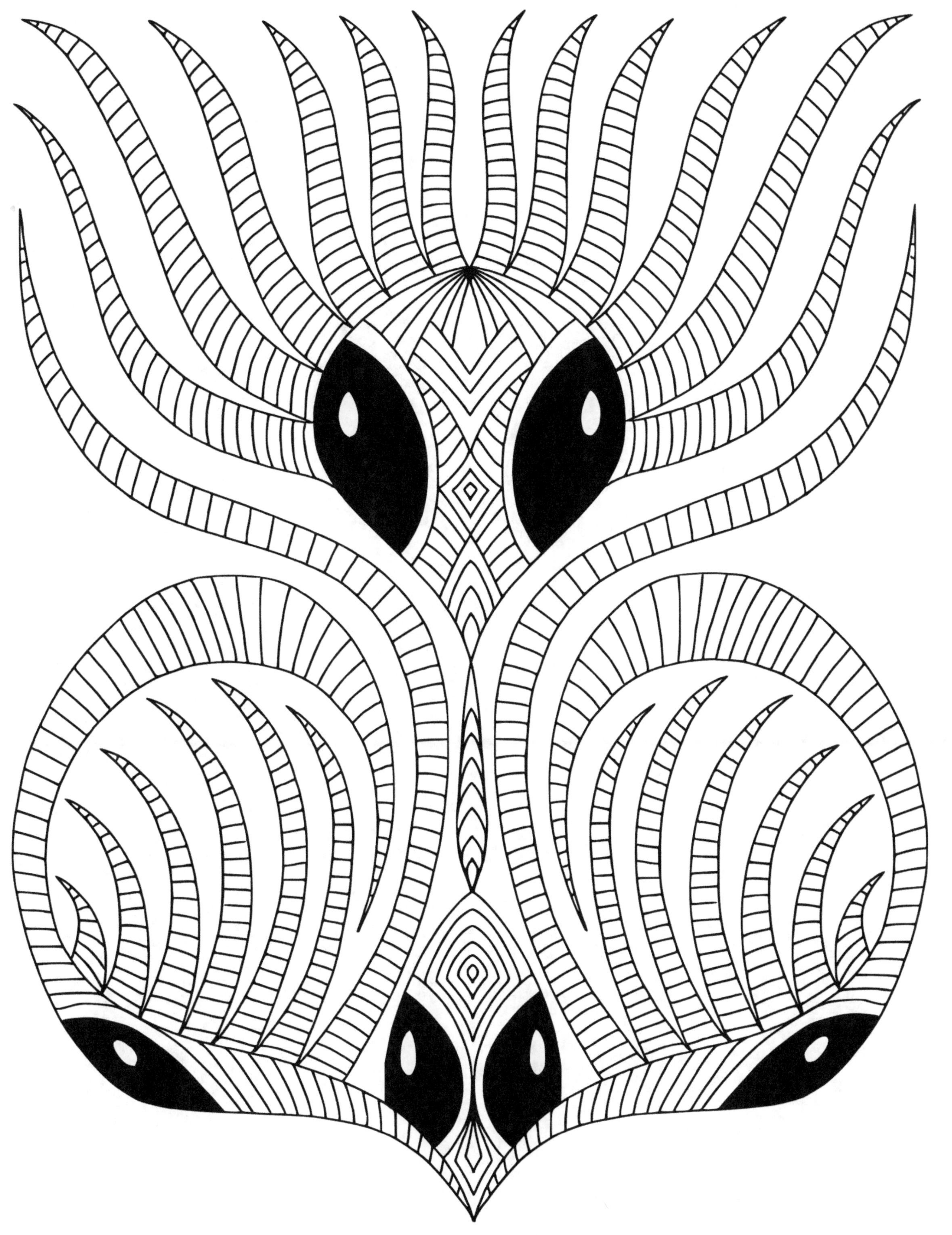

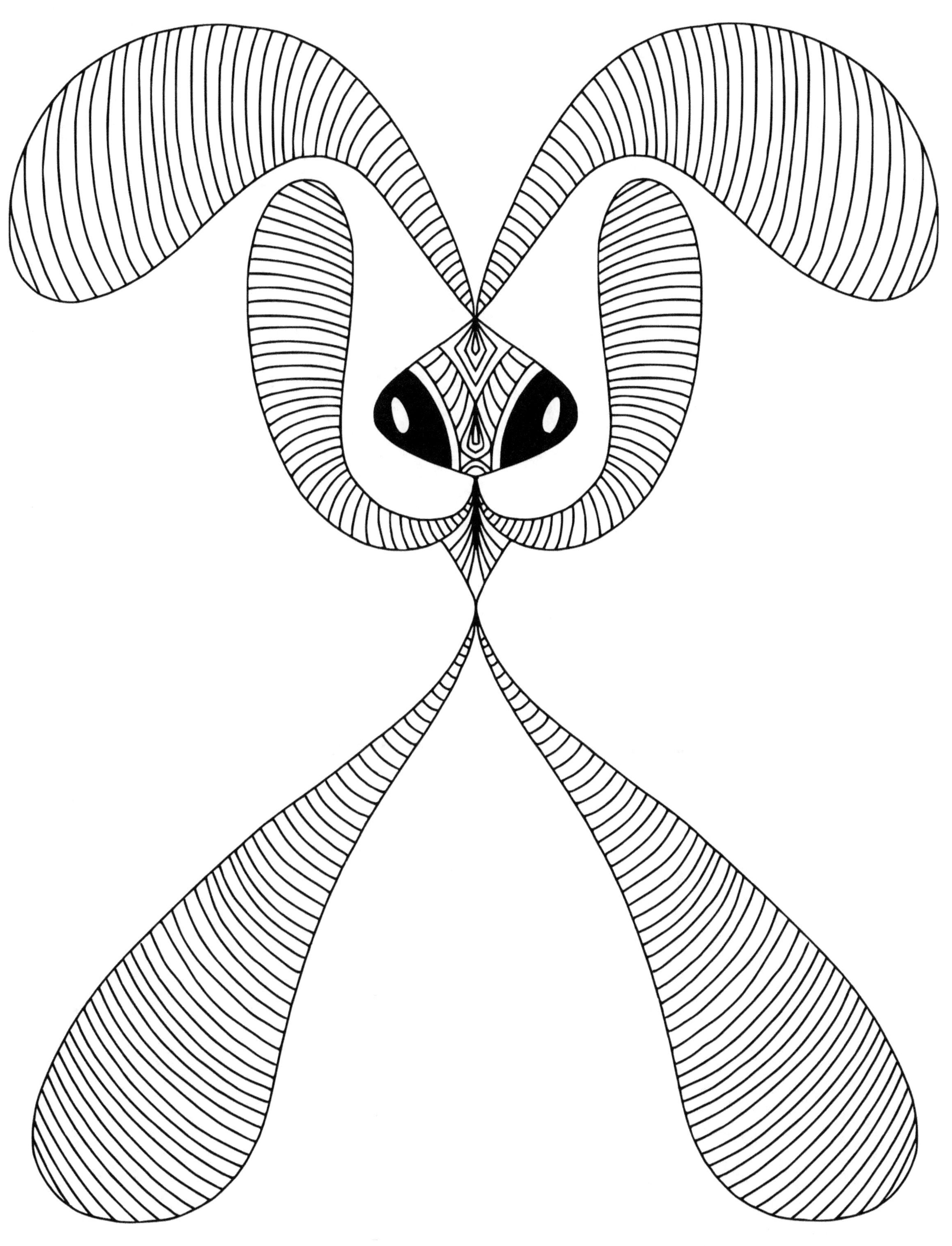

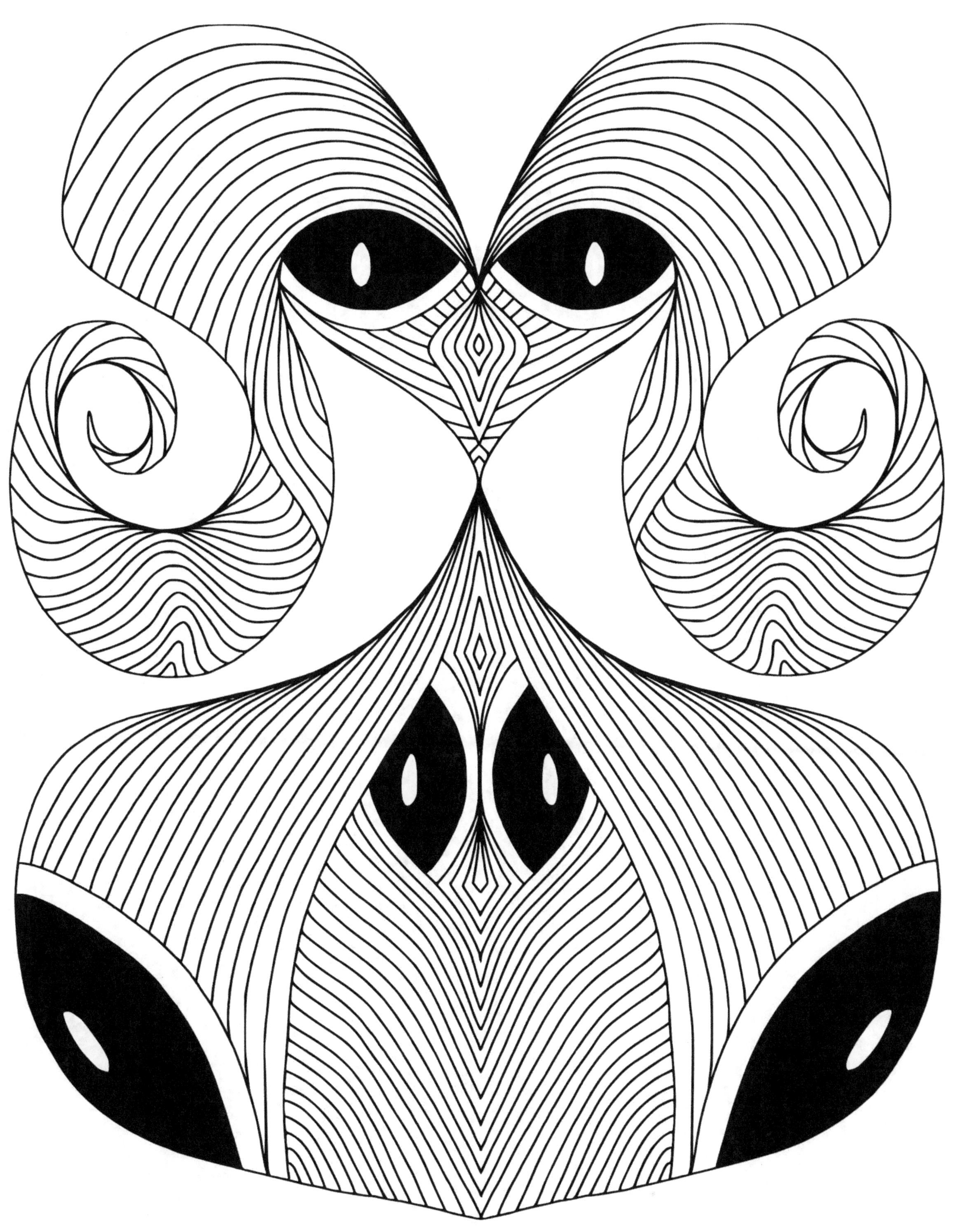

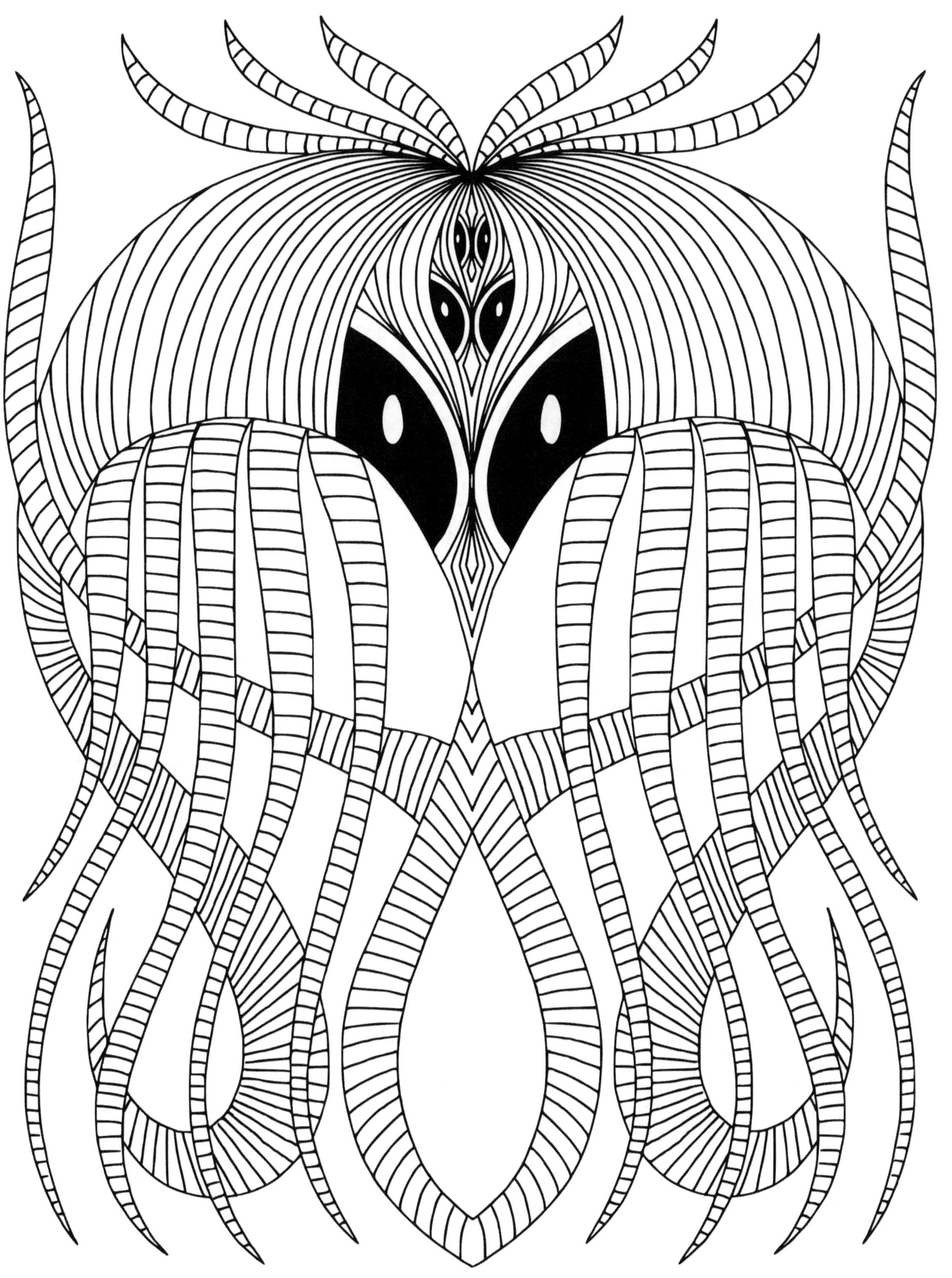

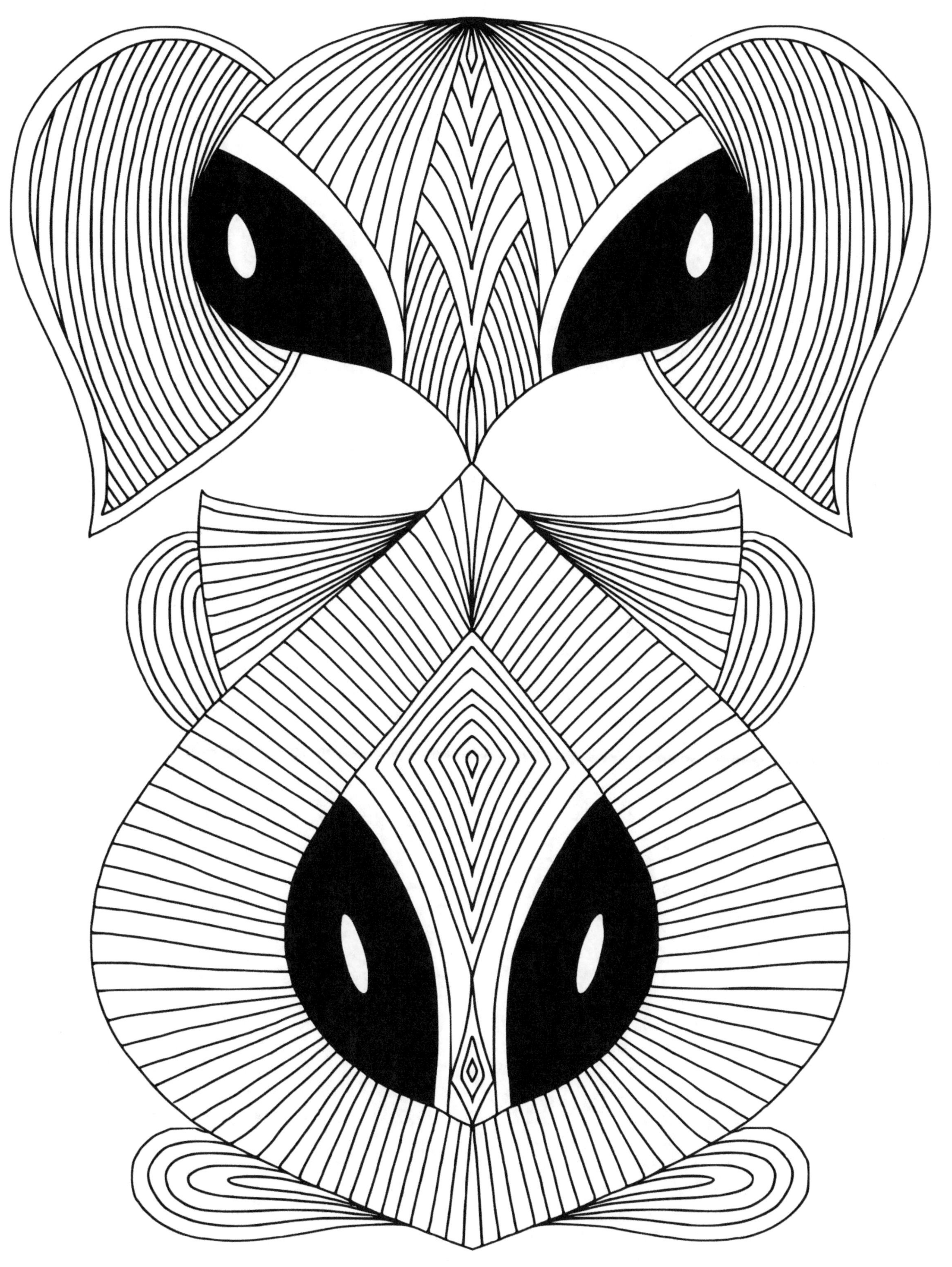

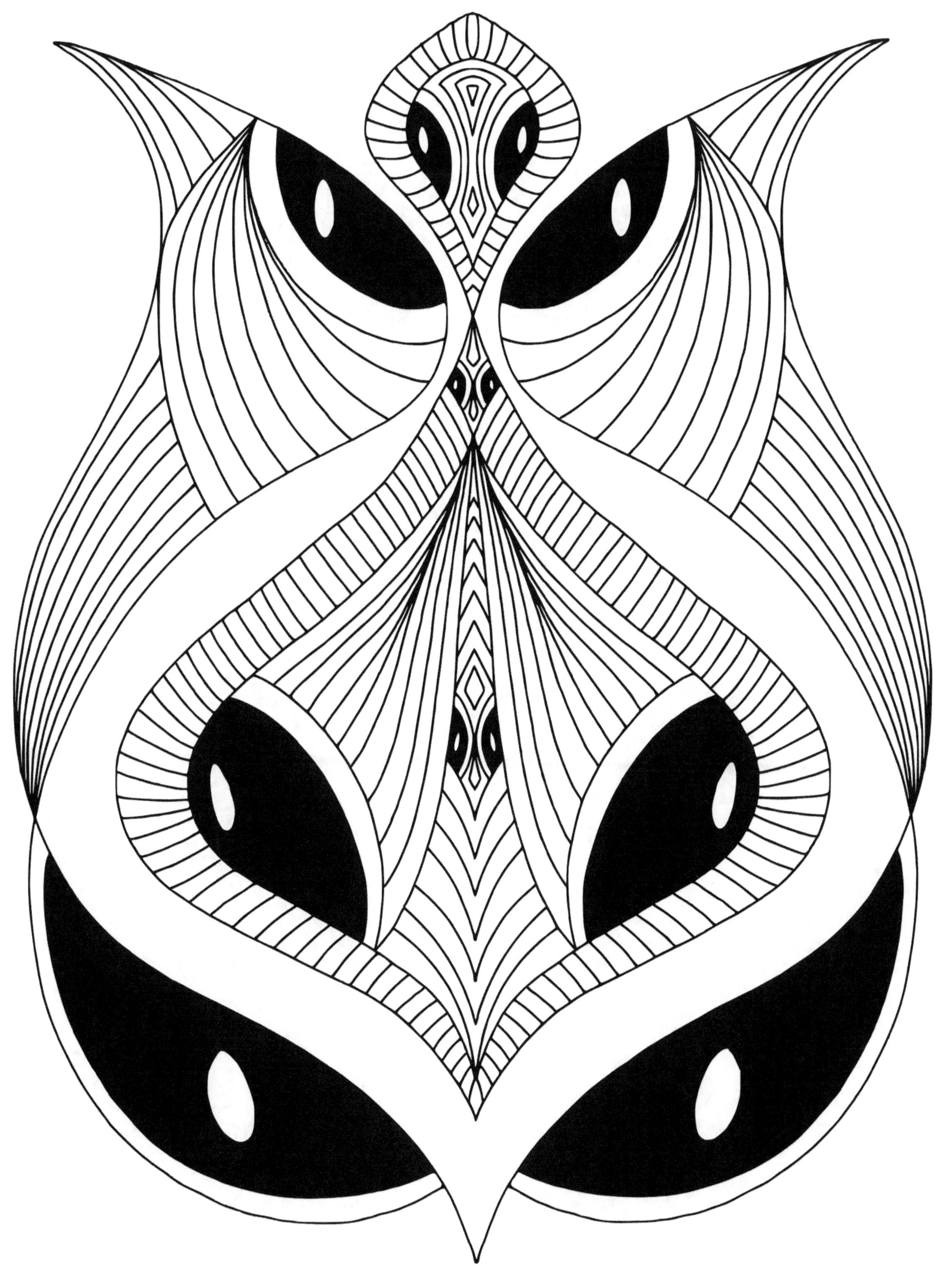

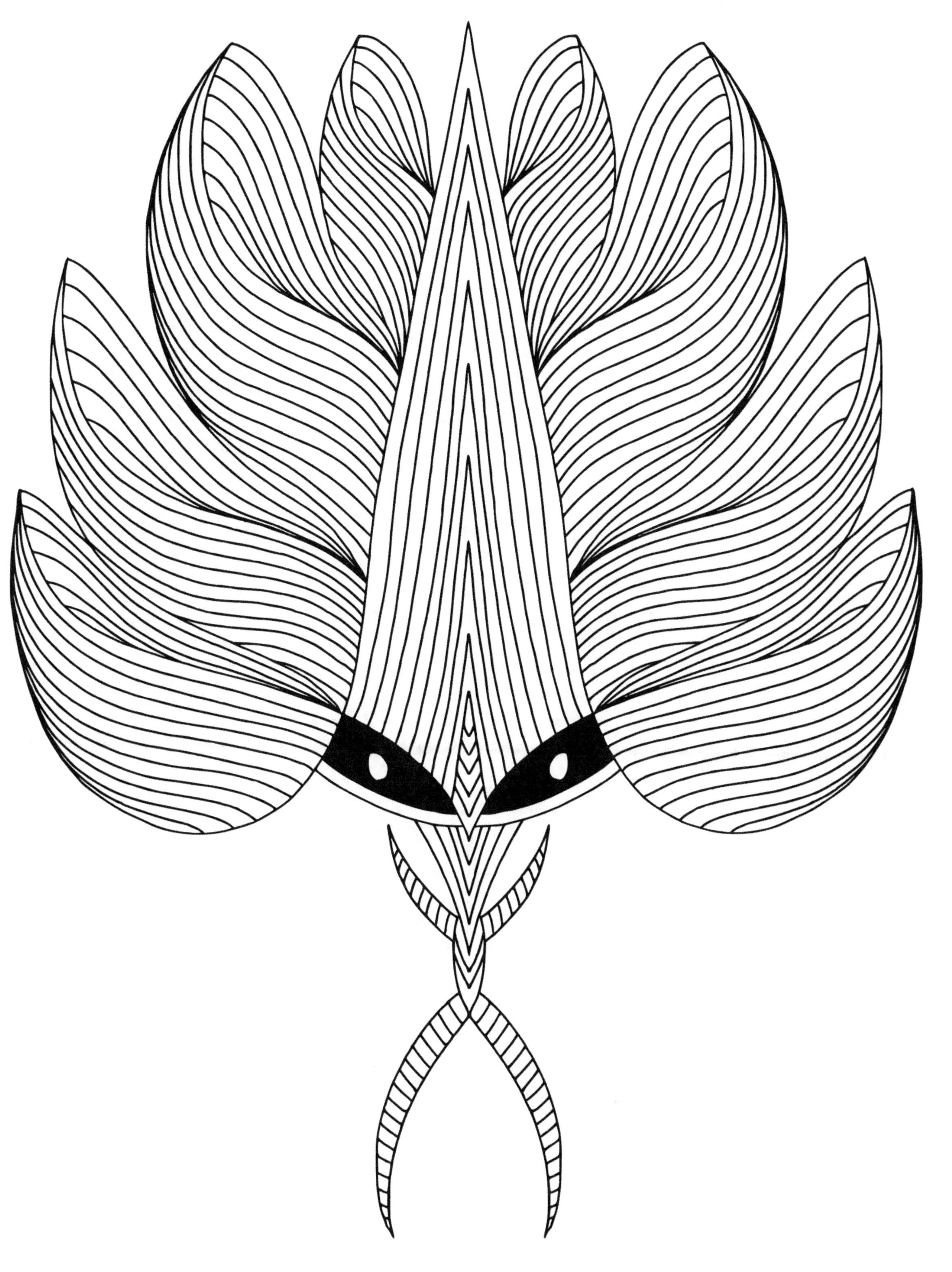

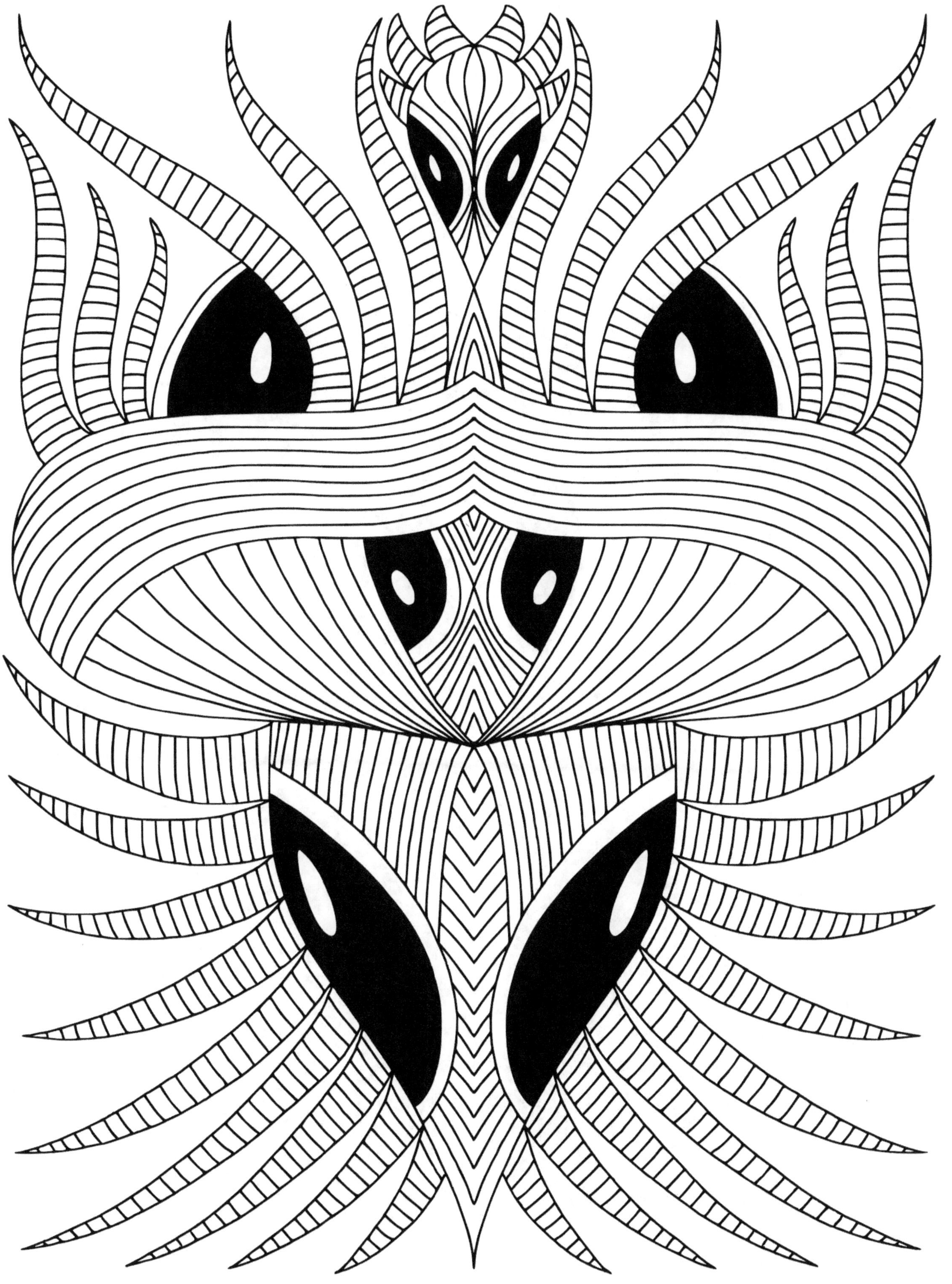

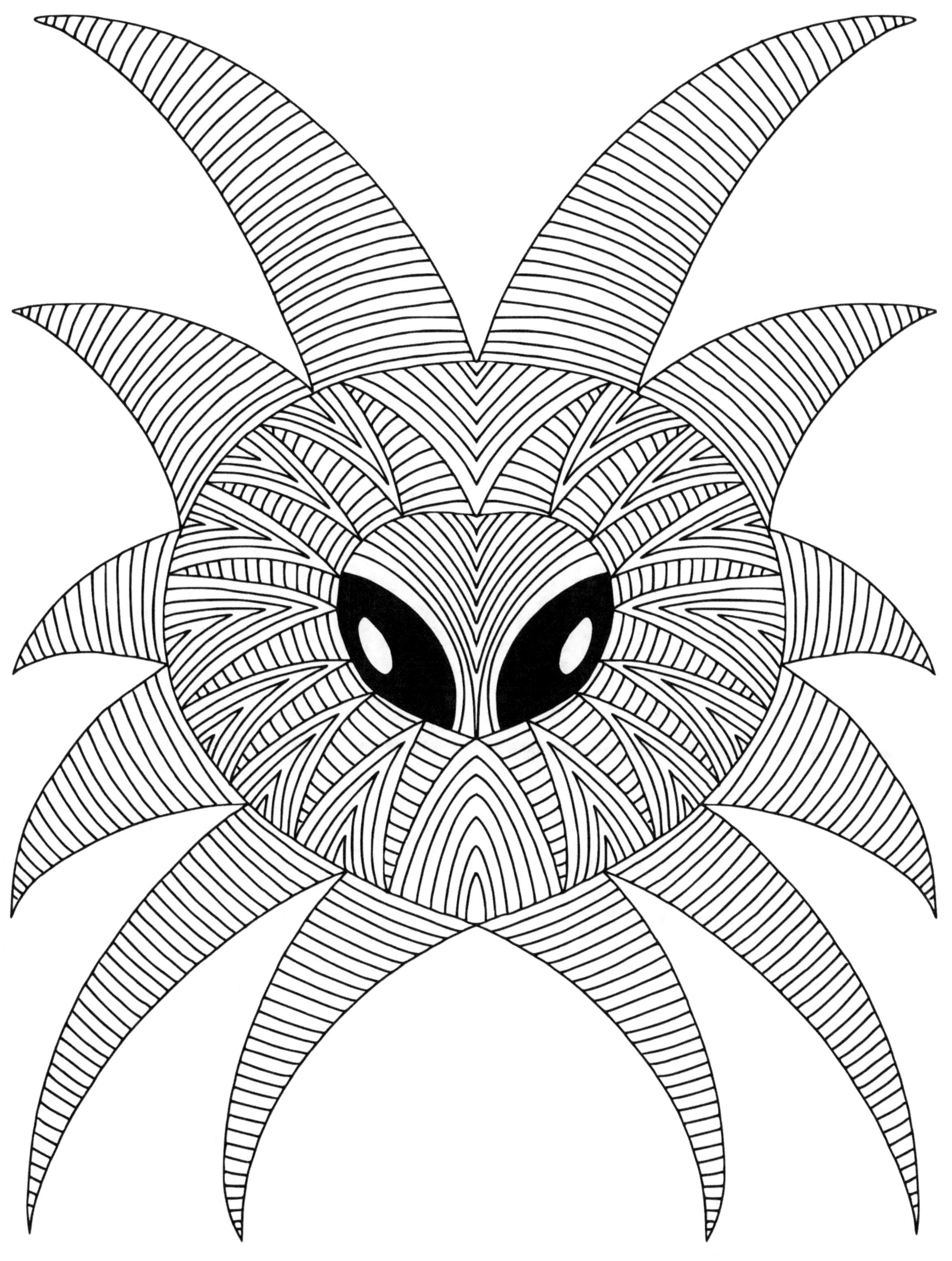

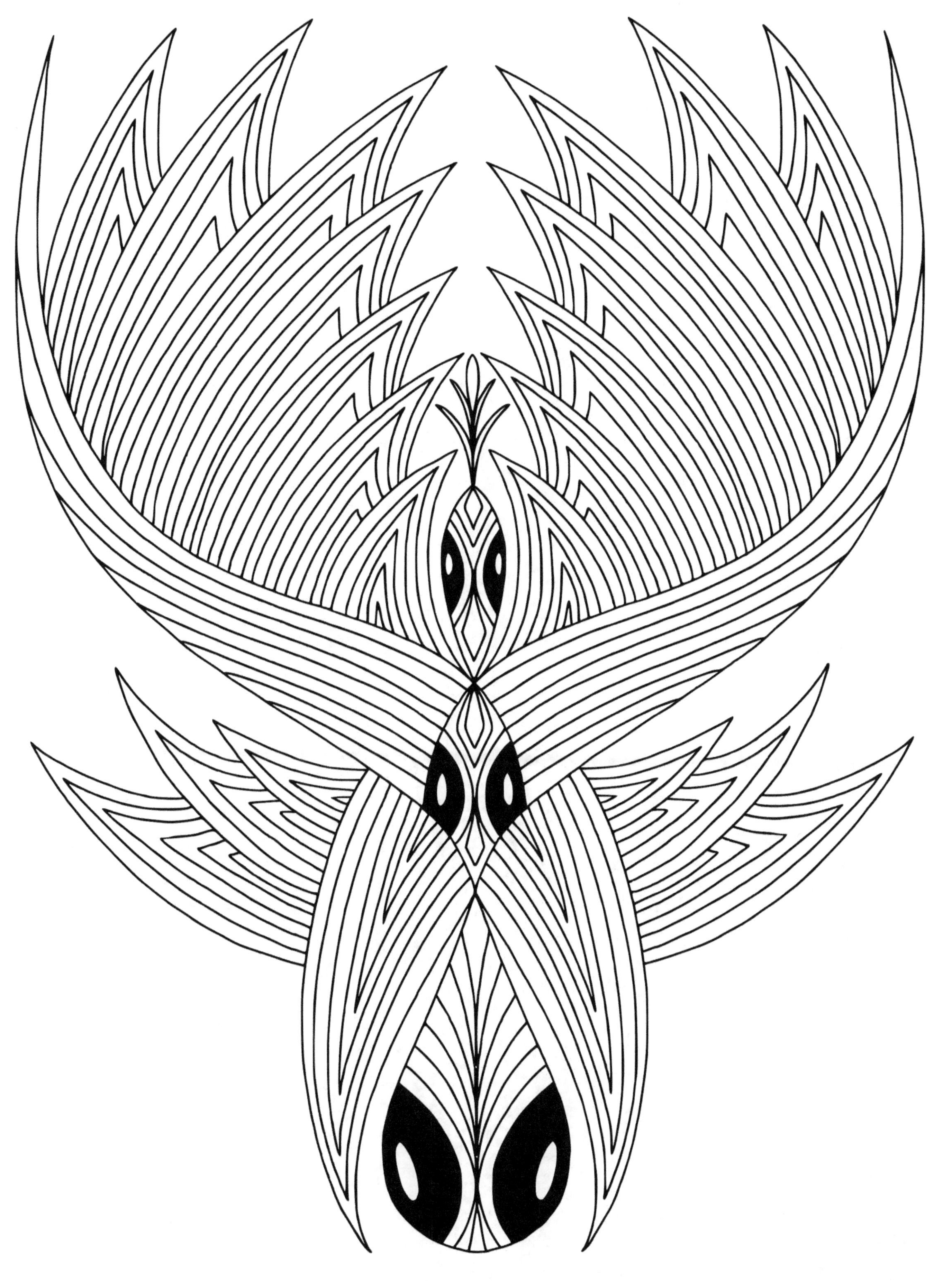

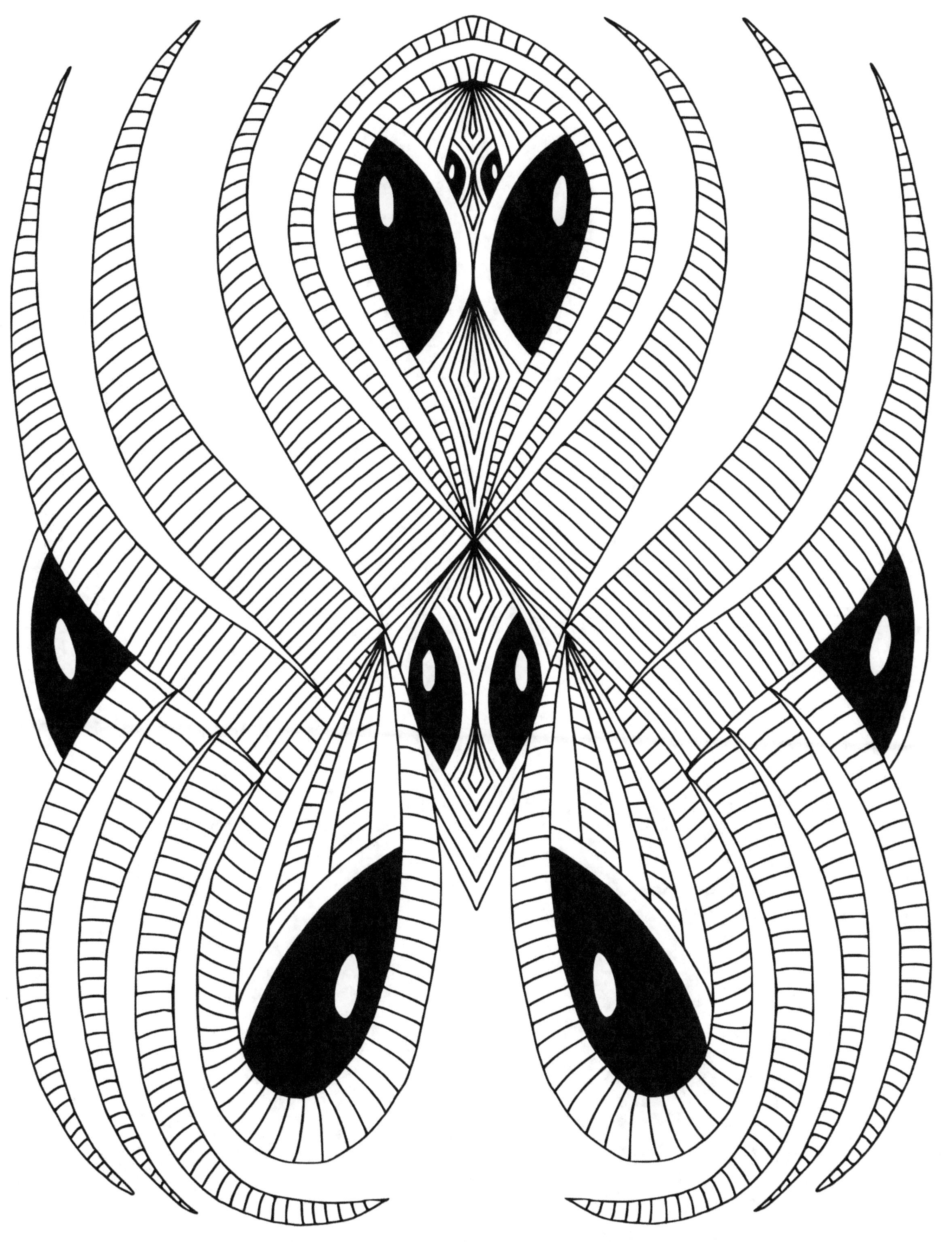

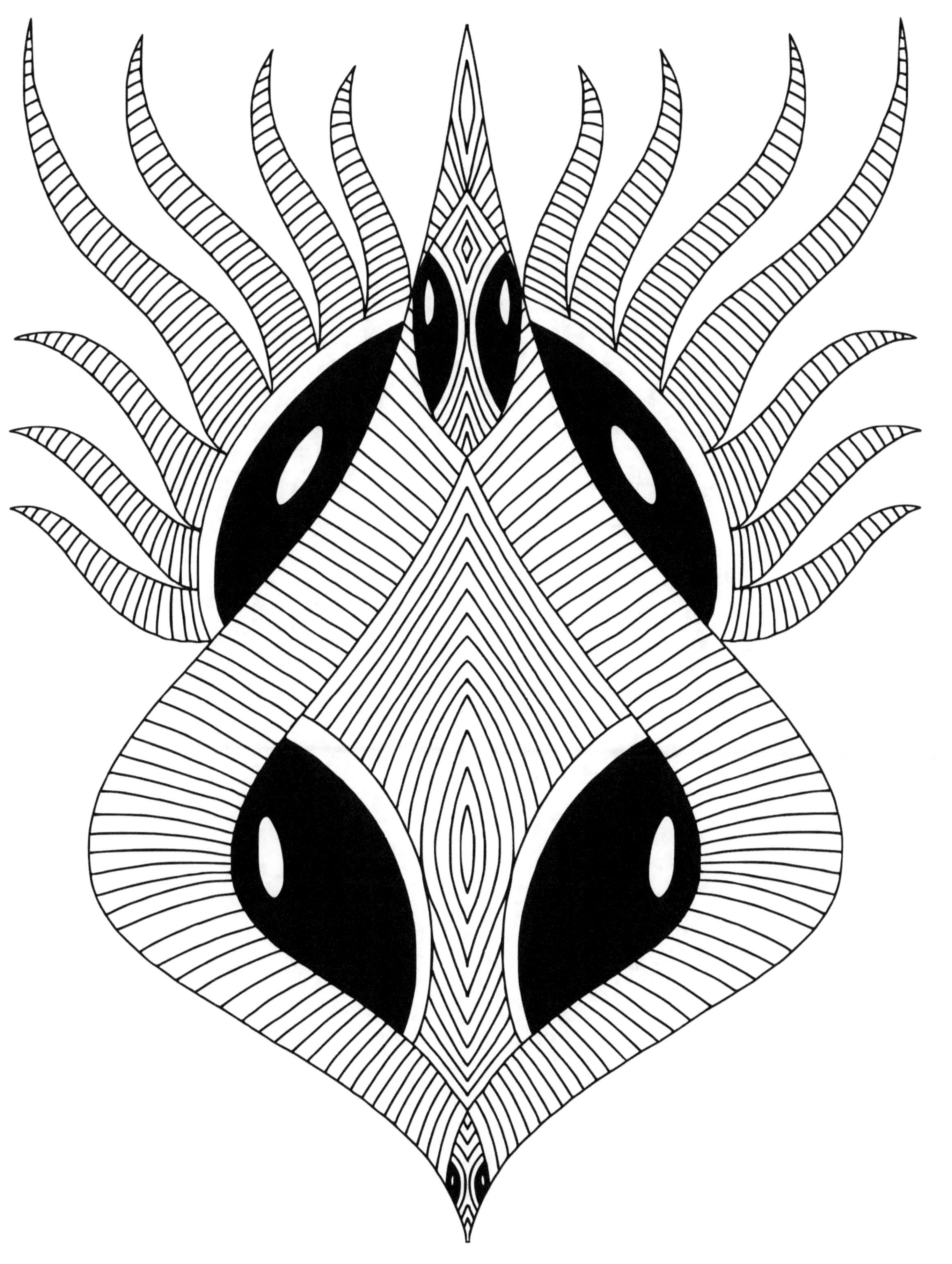

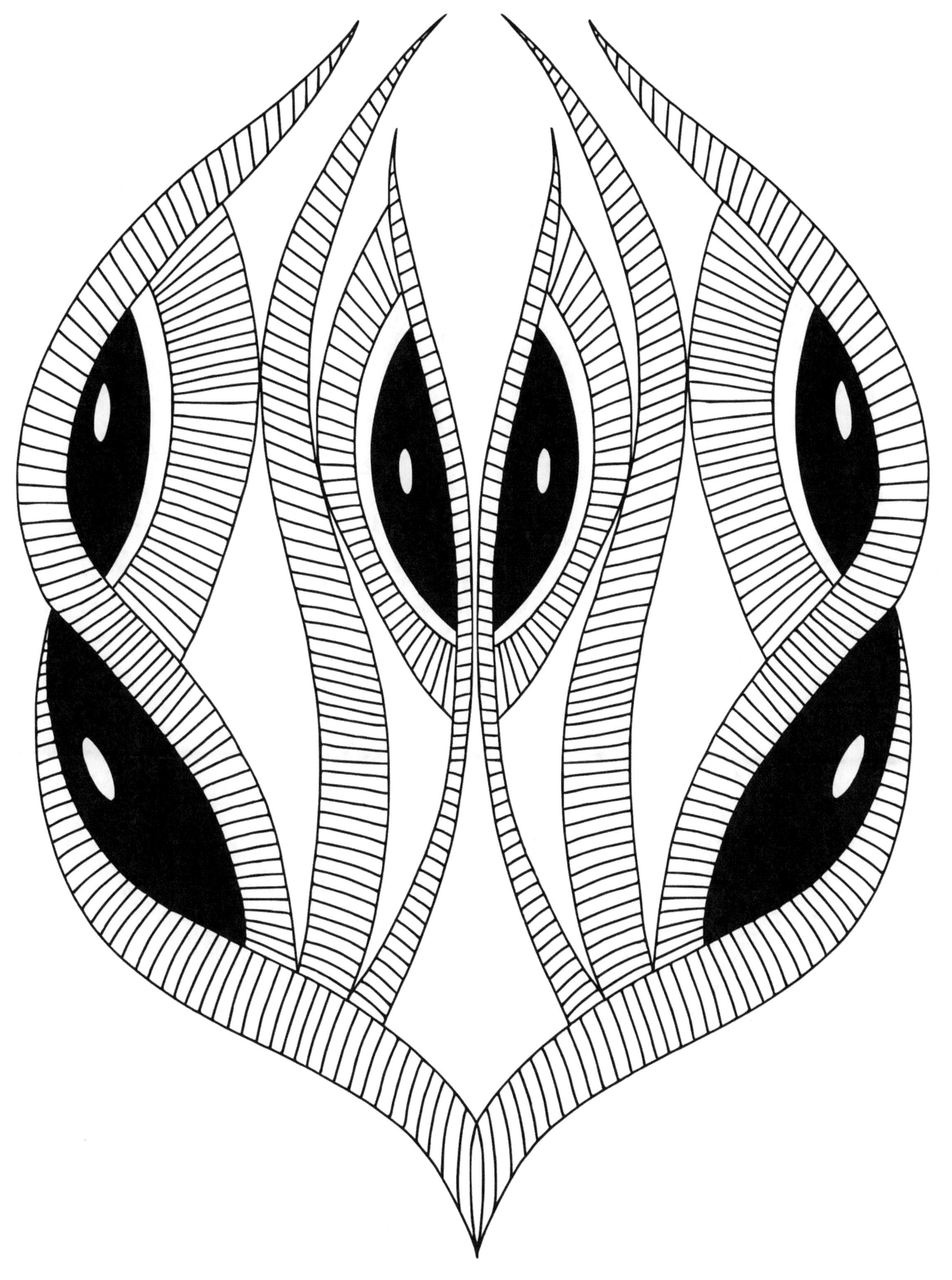

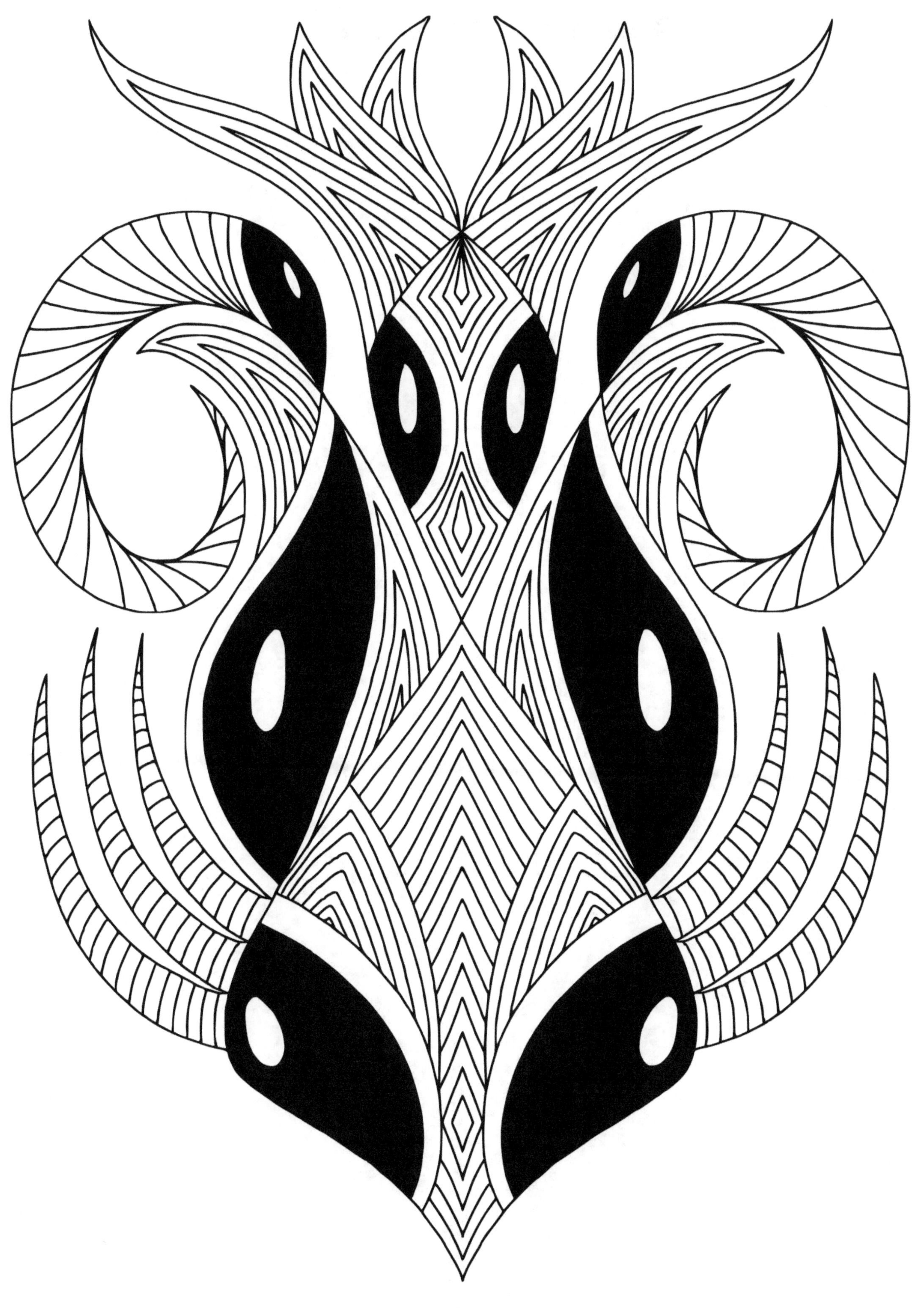

Bonus Upside Down versions......

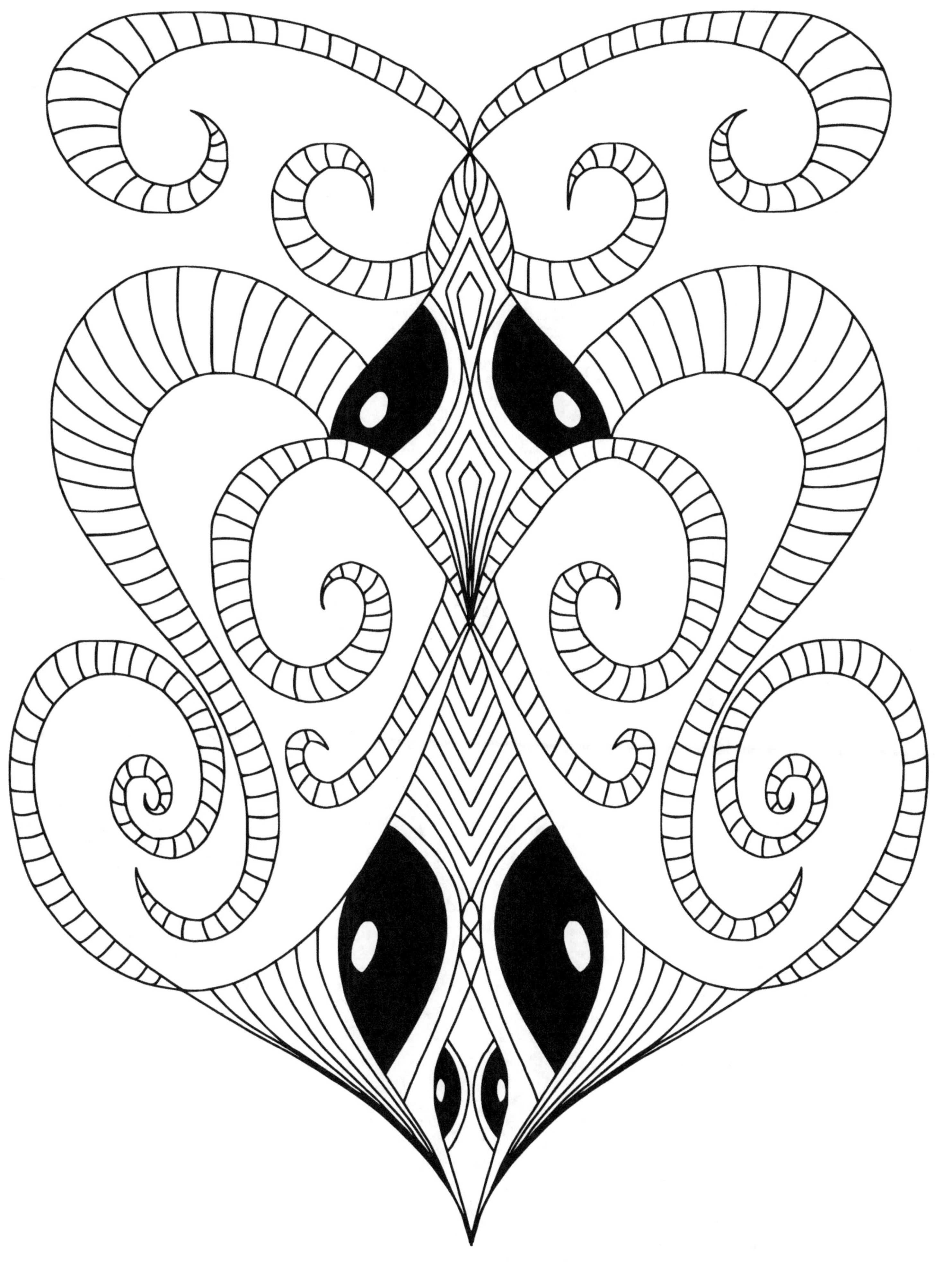

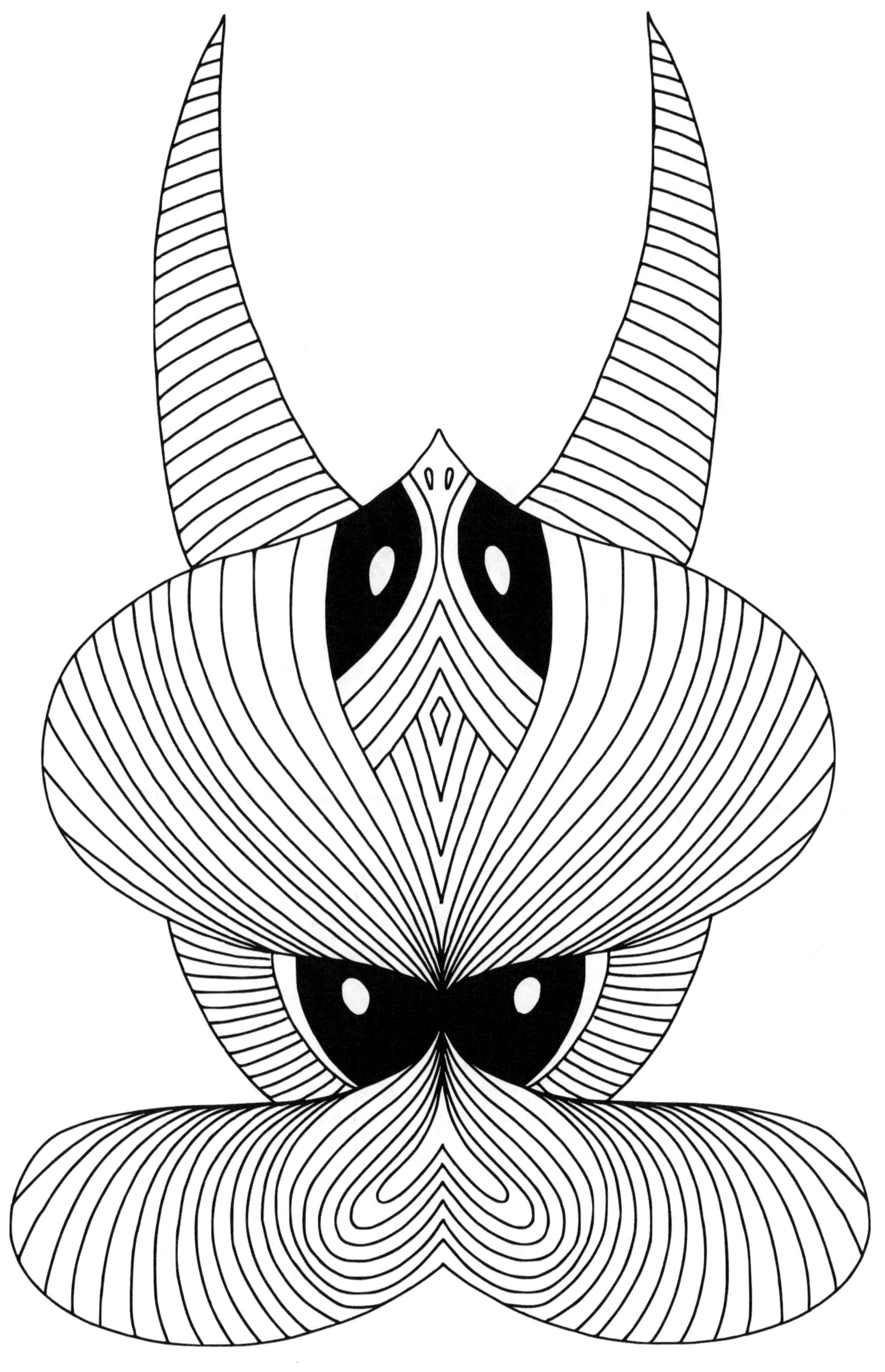

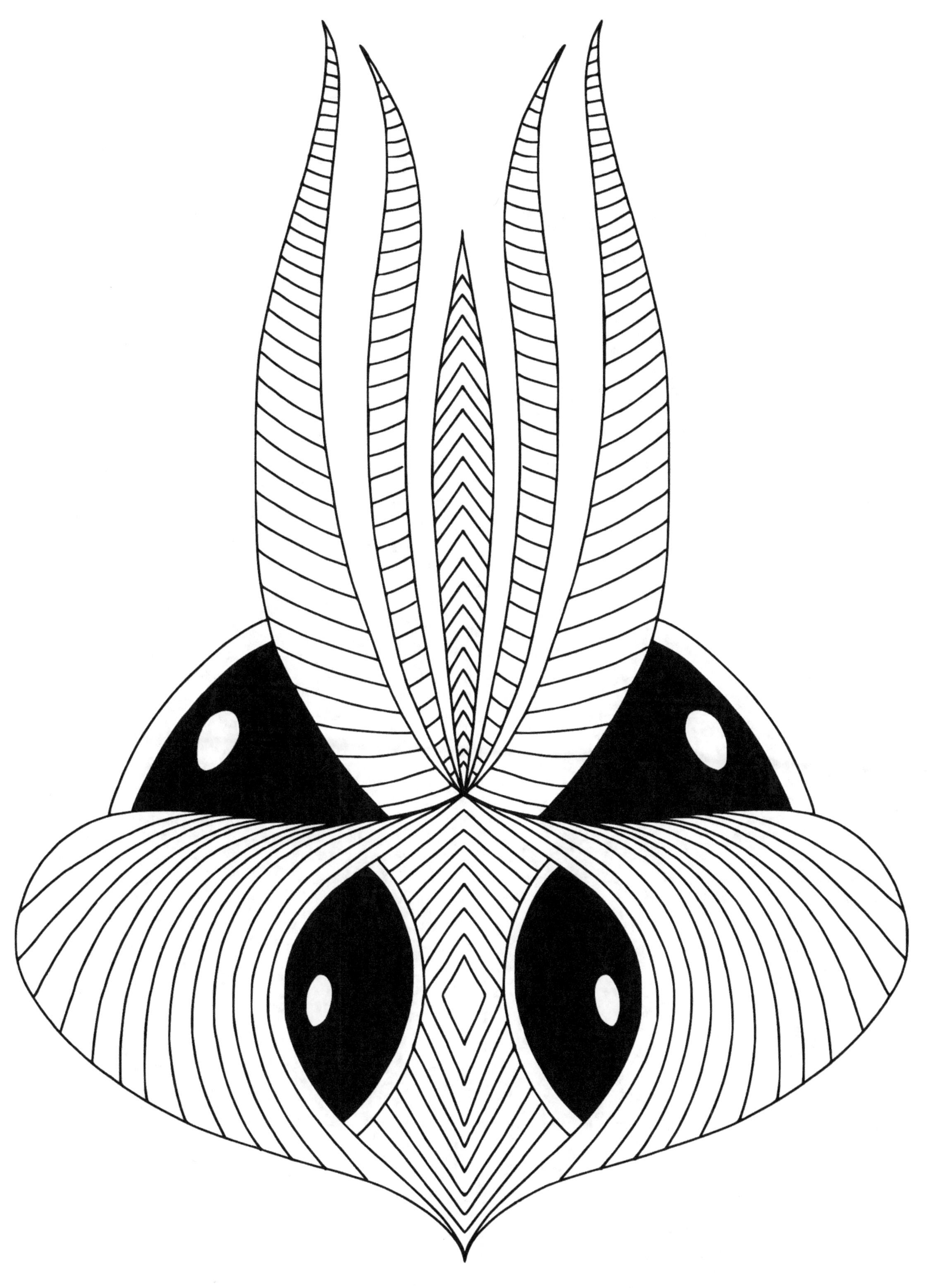

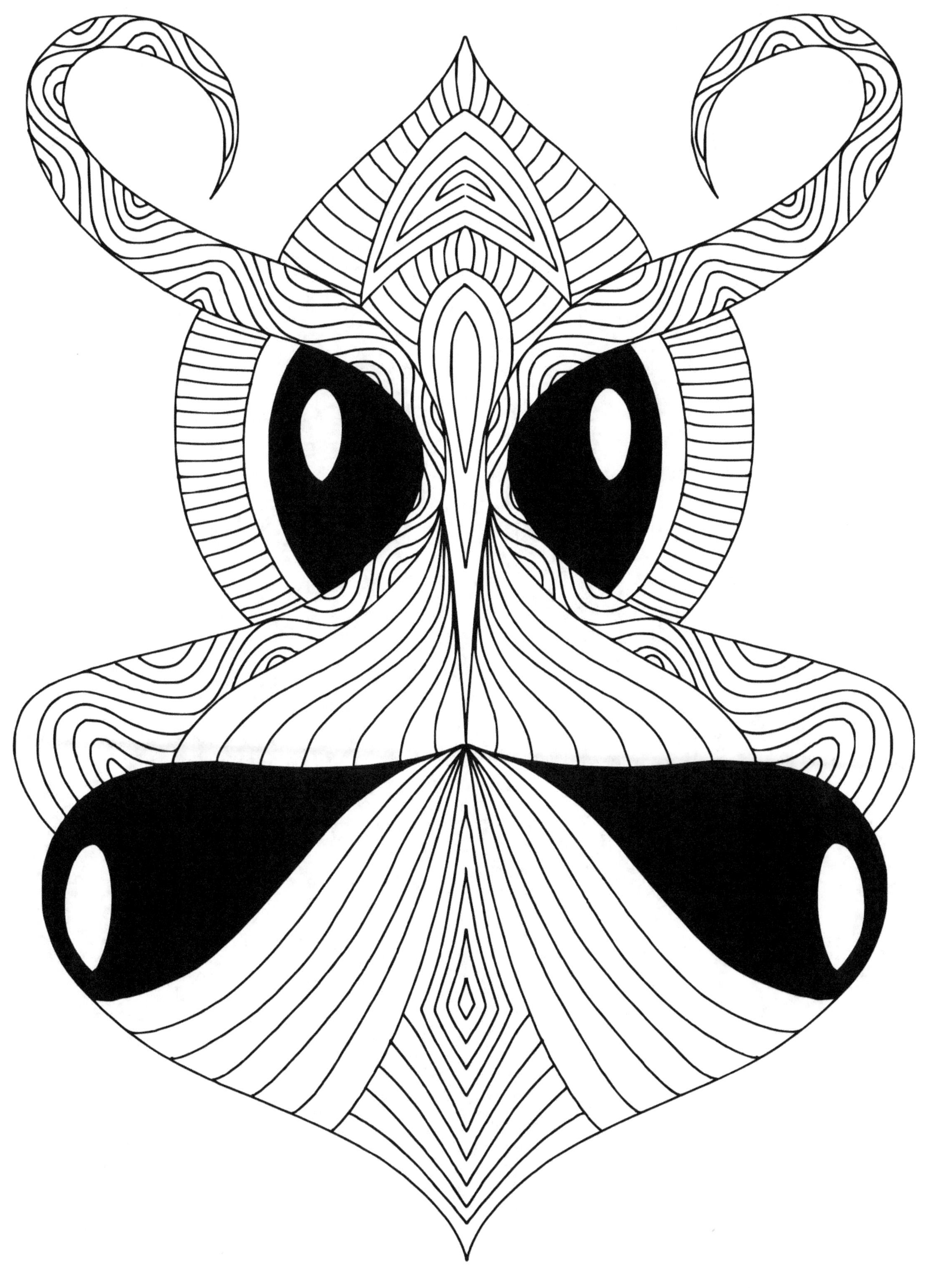

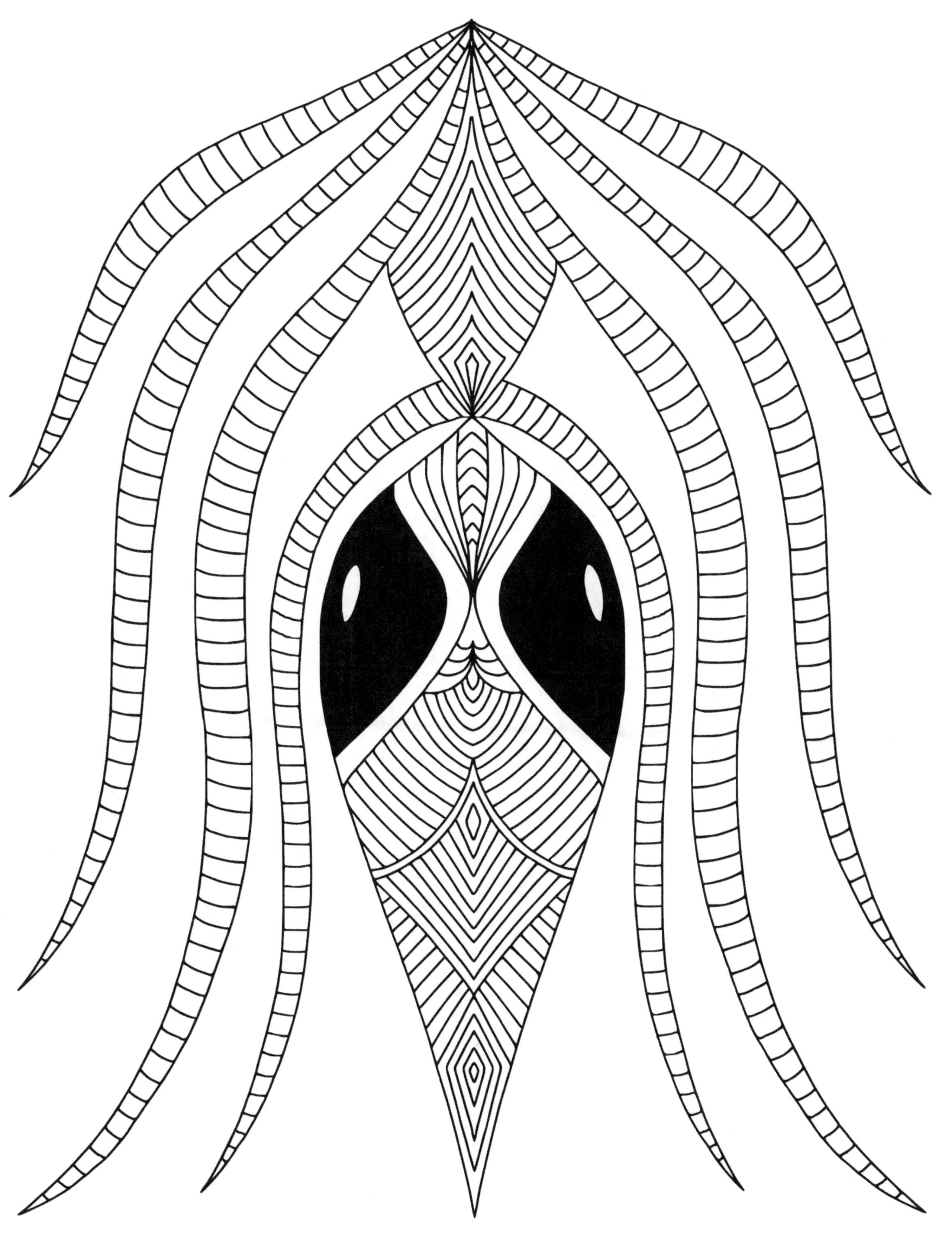

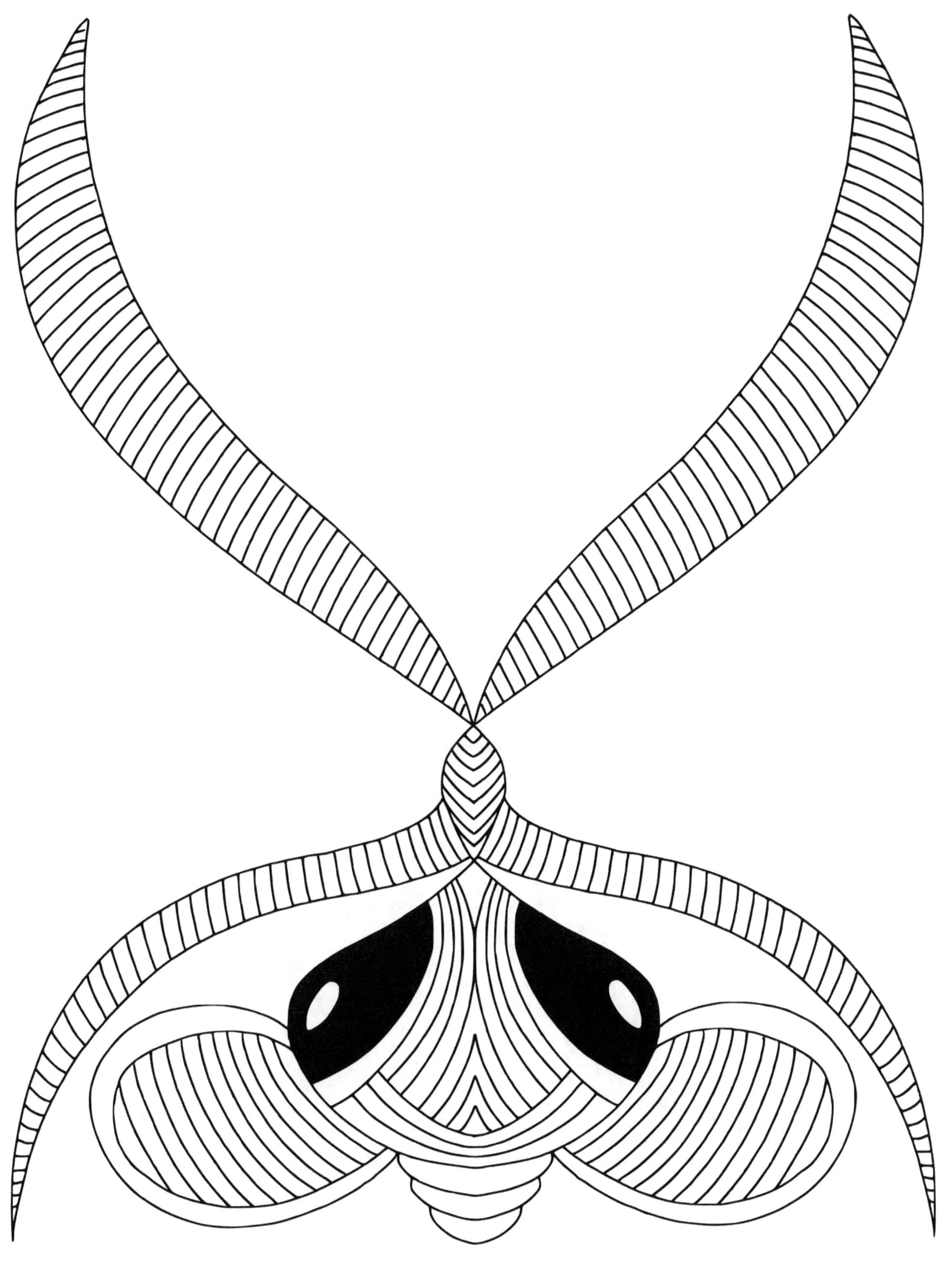

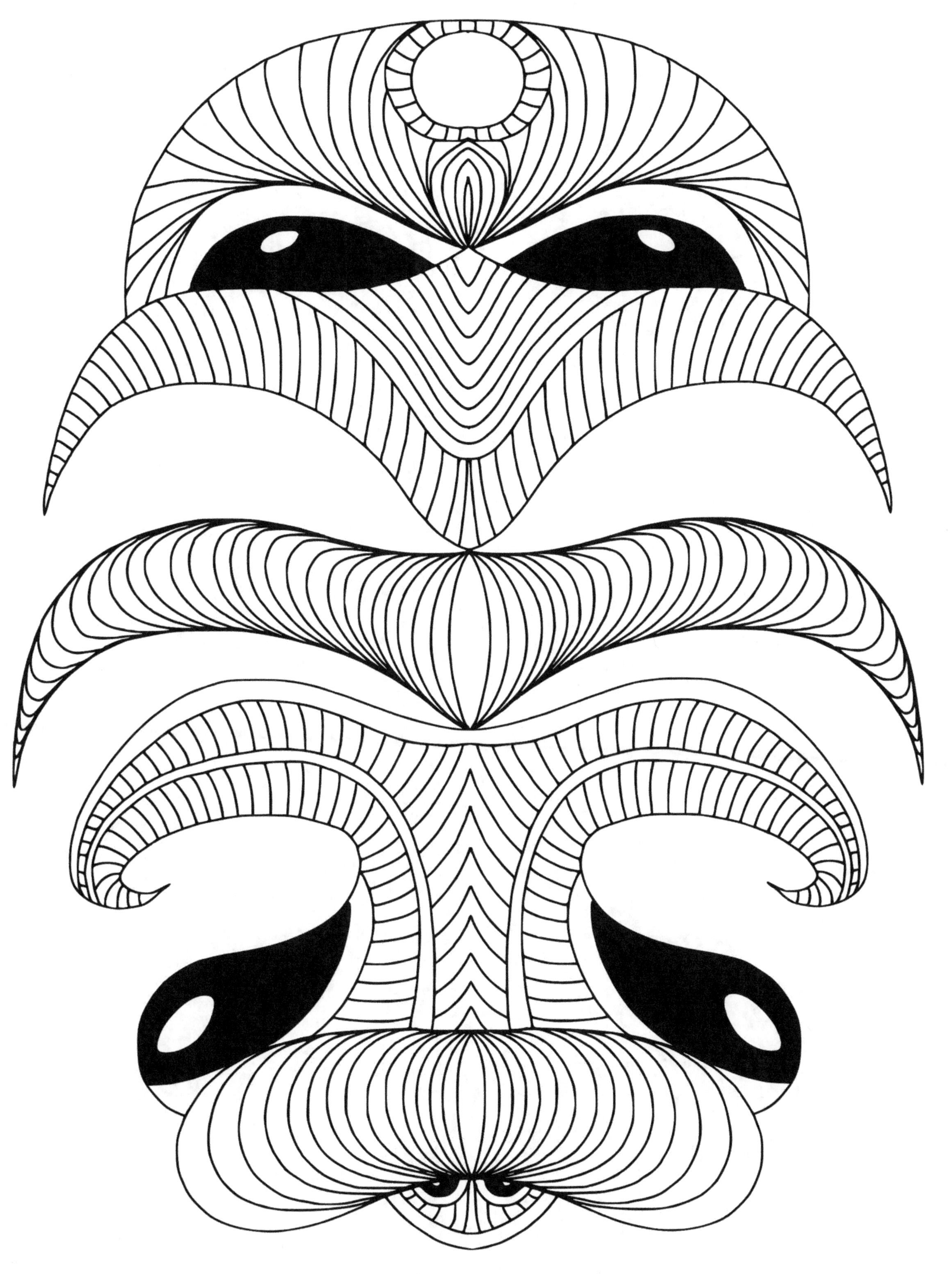

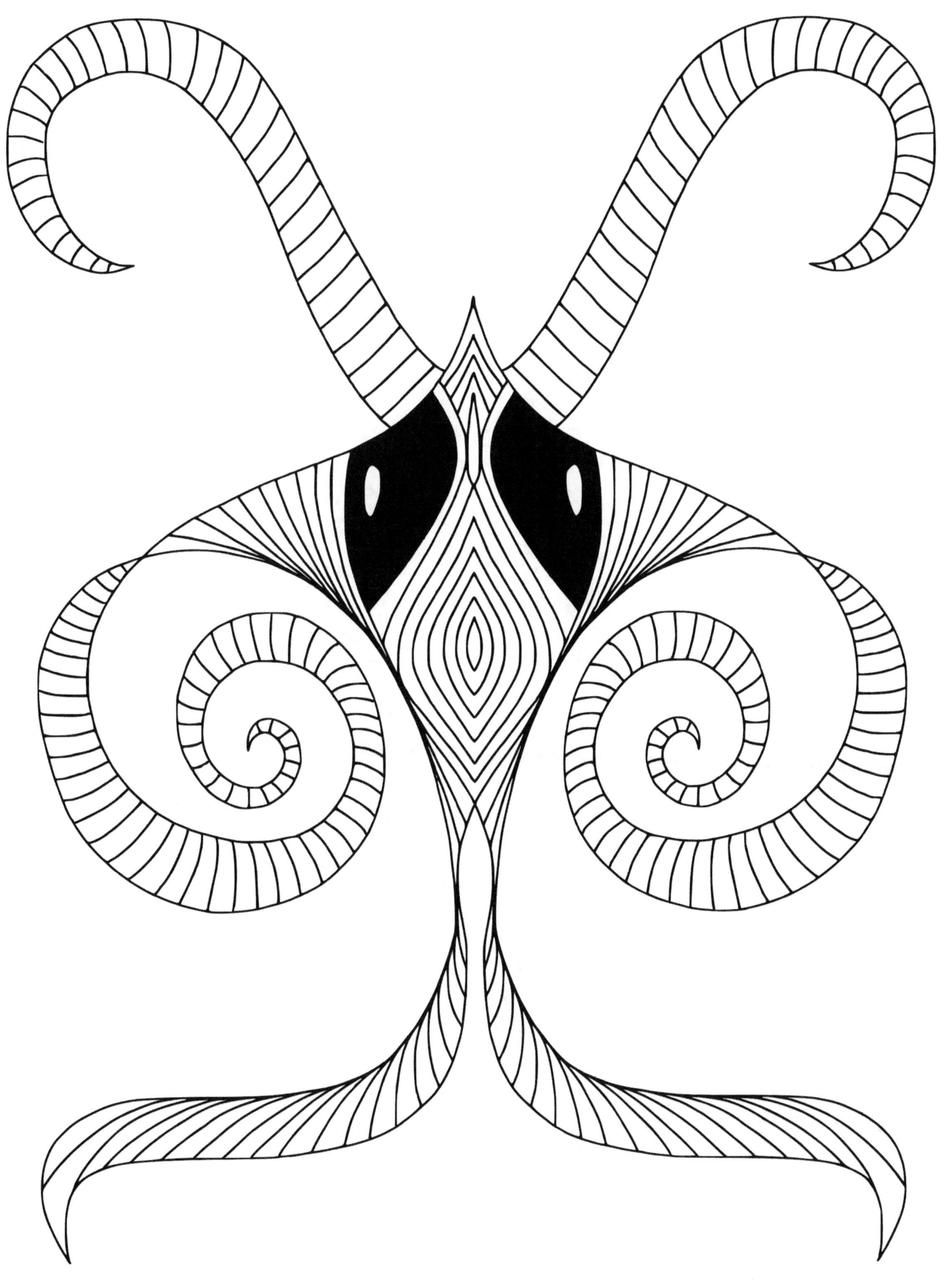

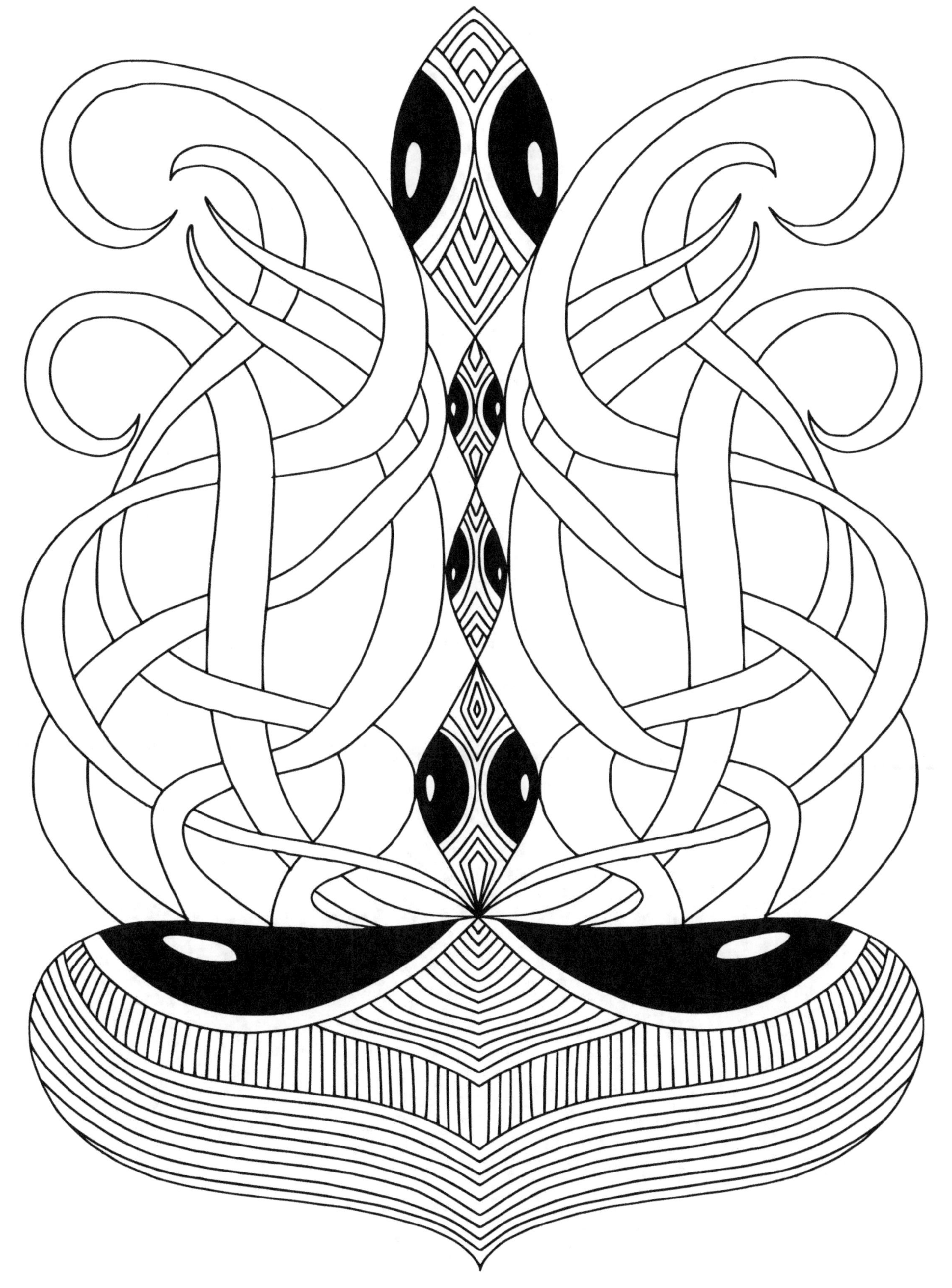

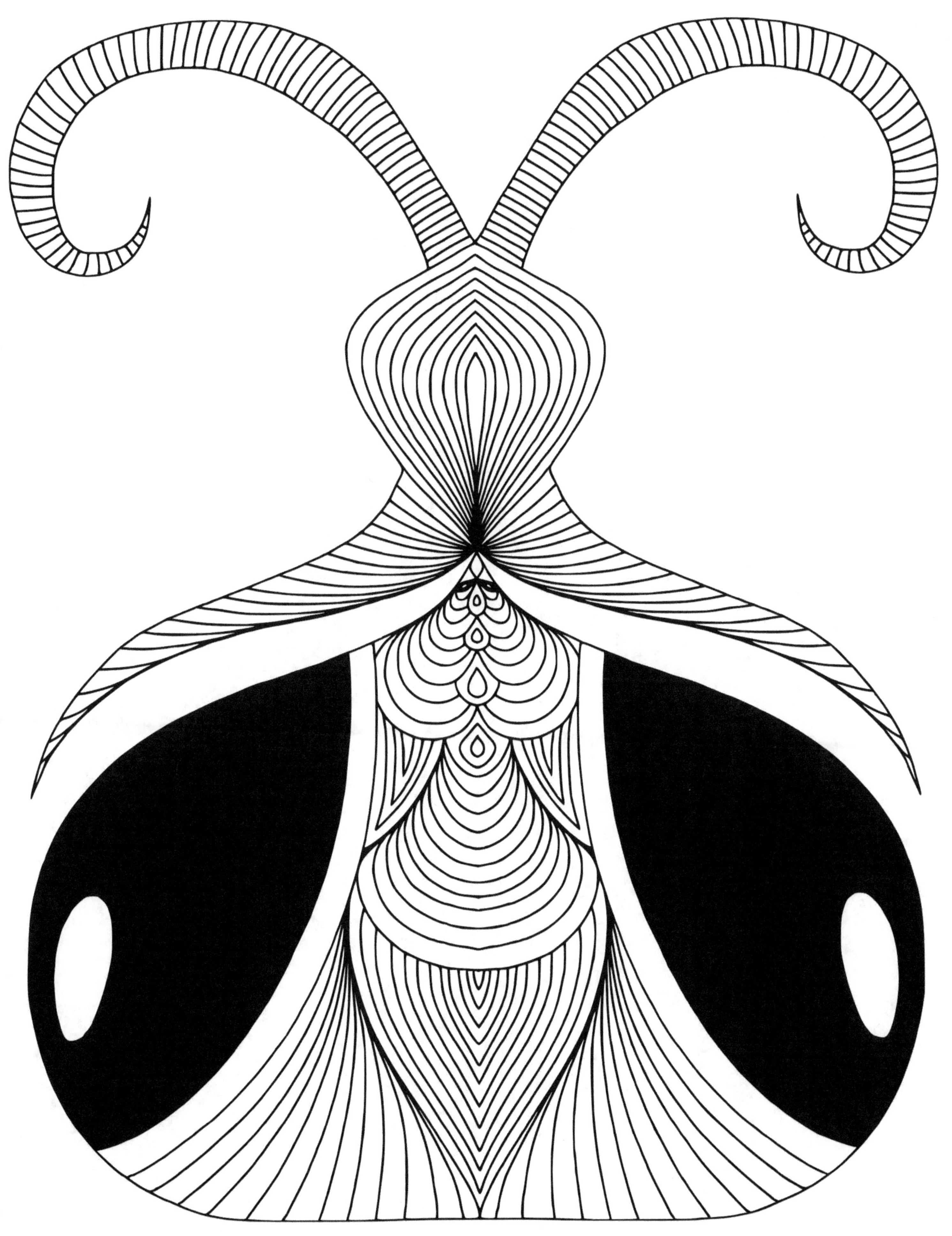

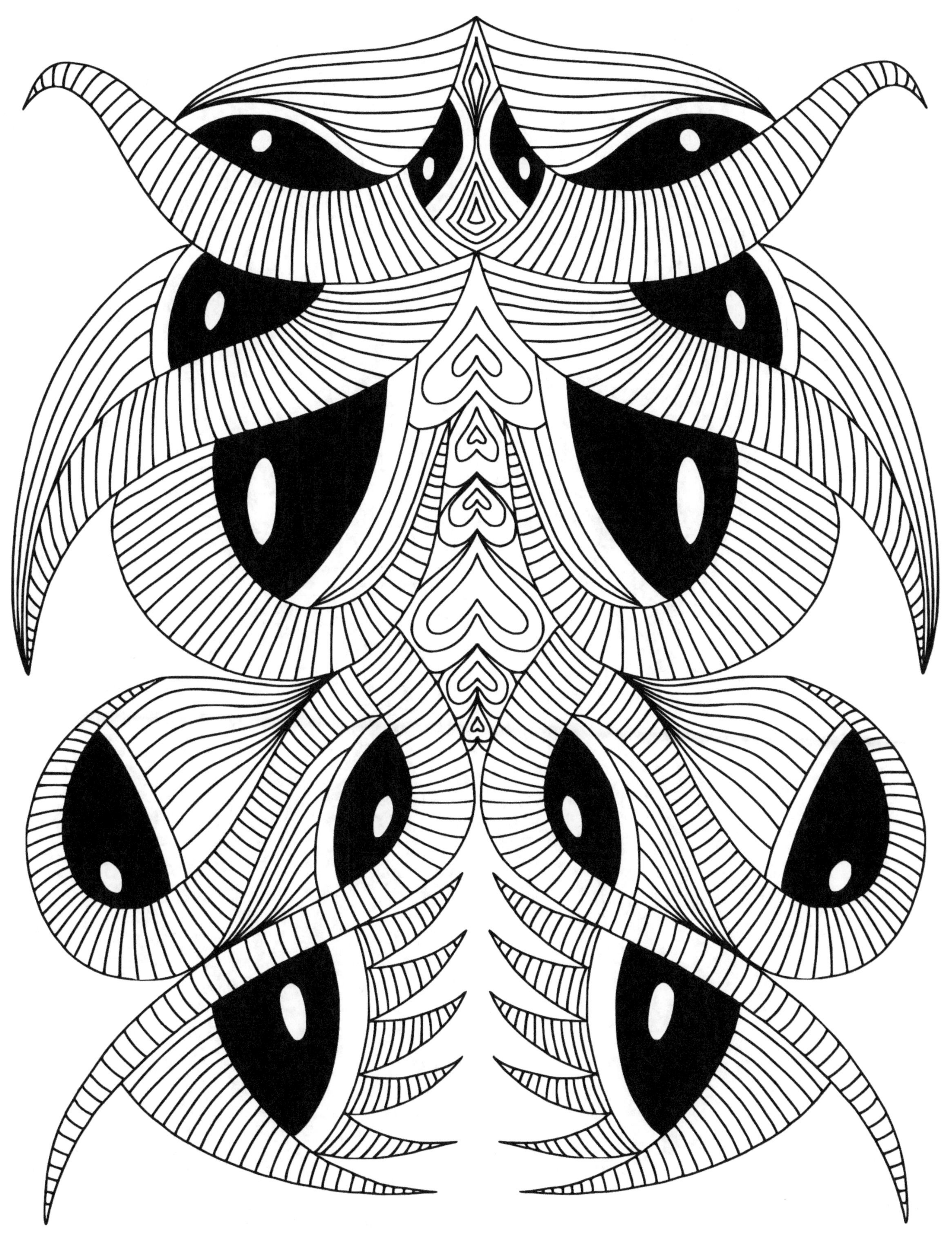

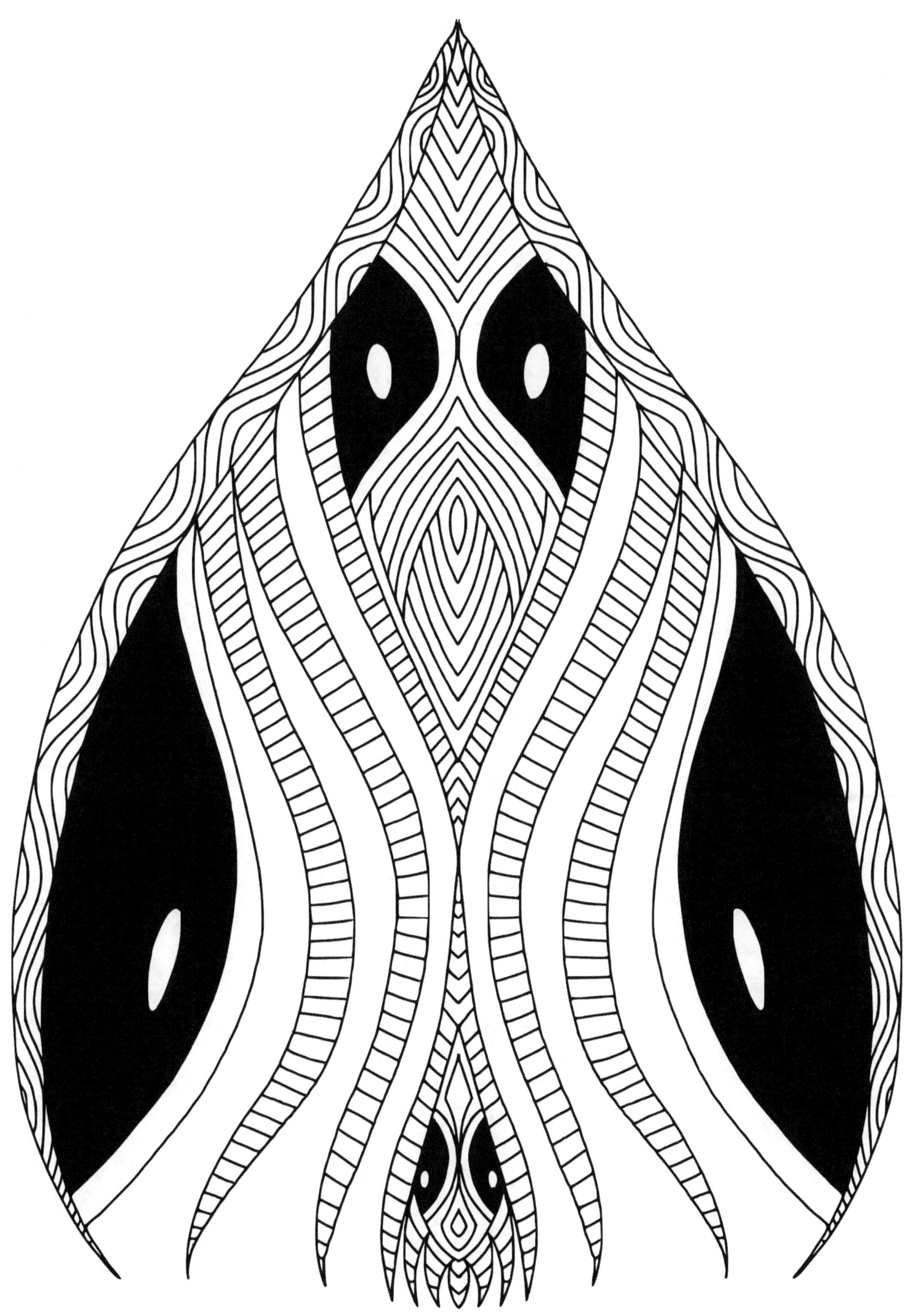

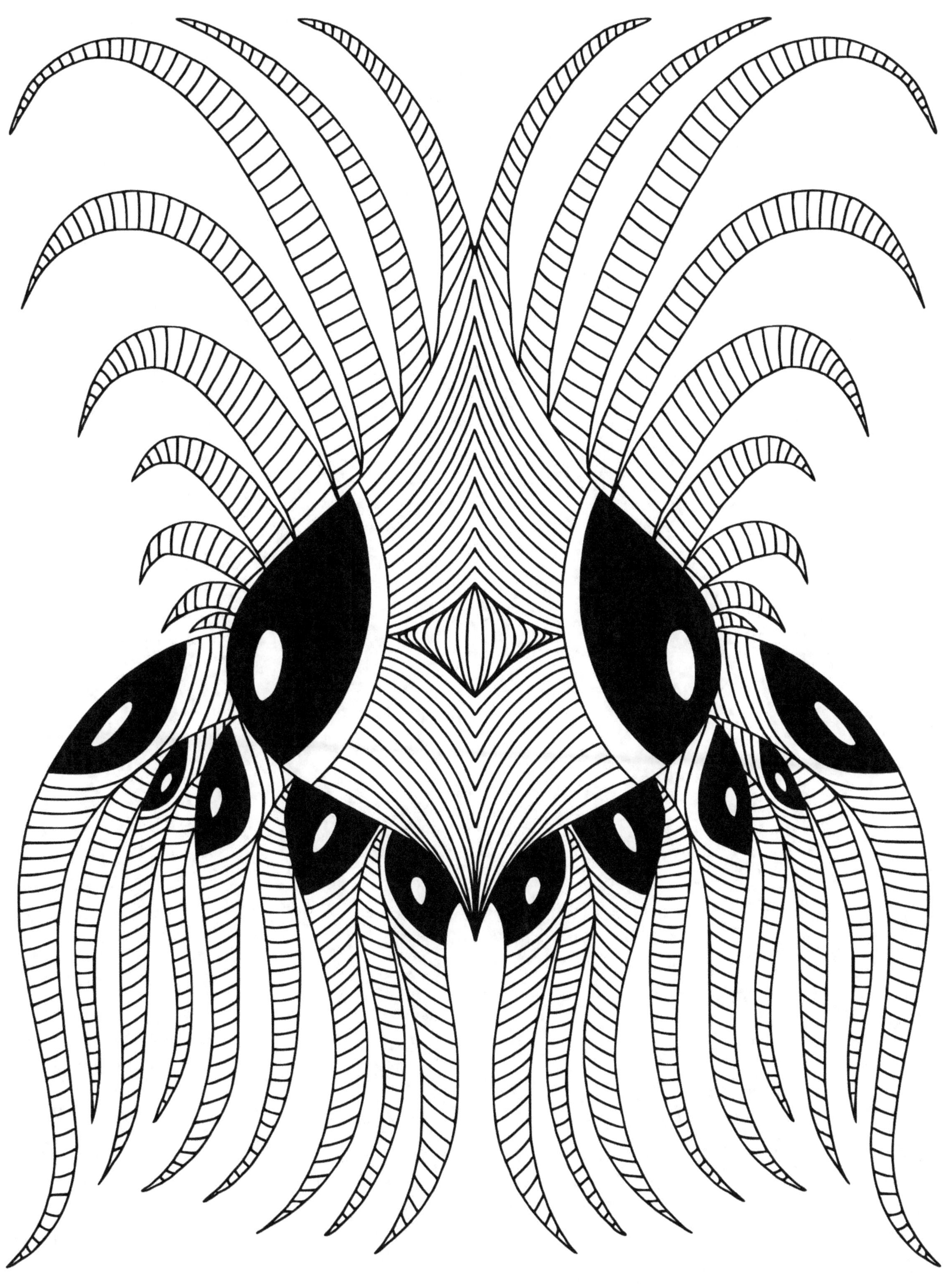

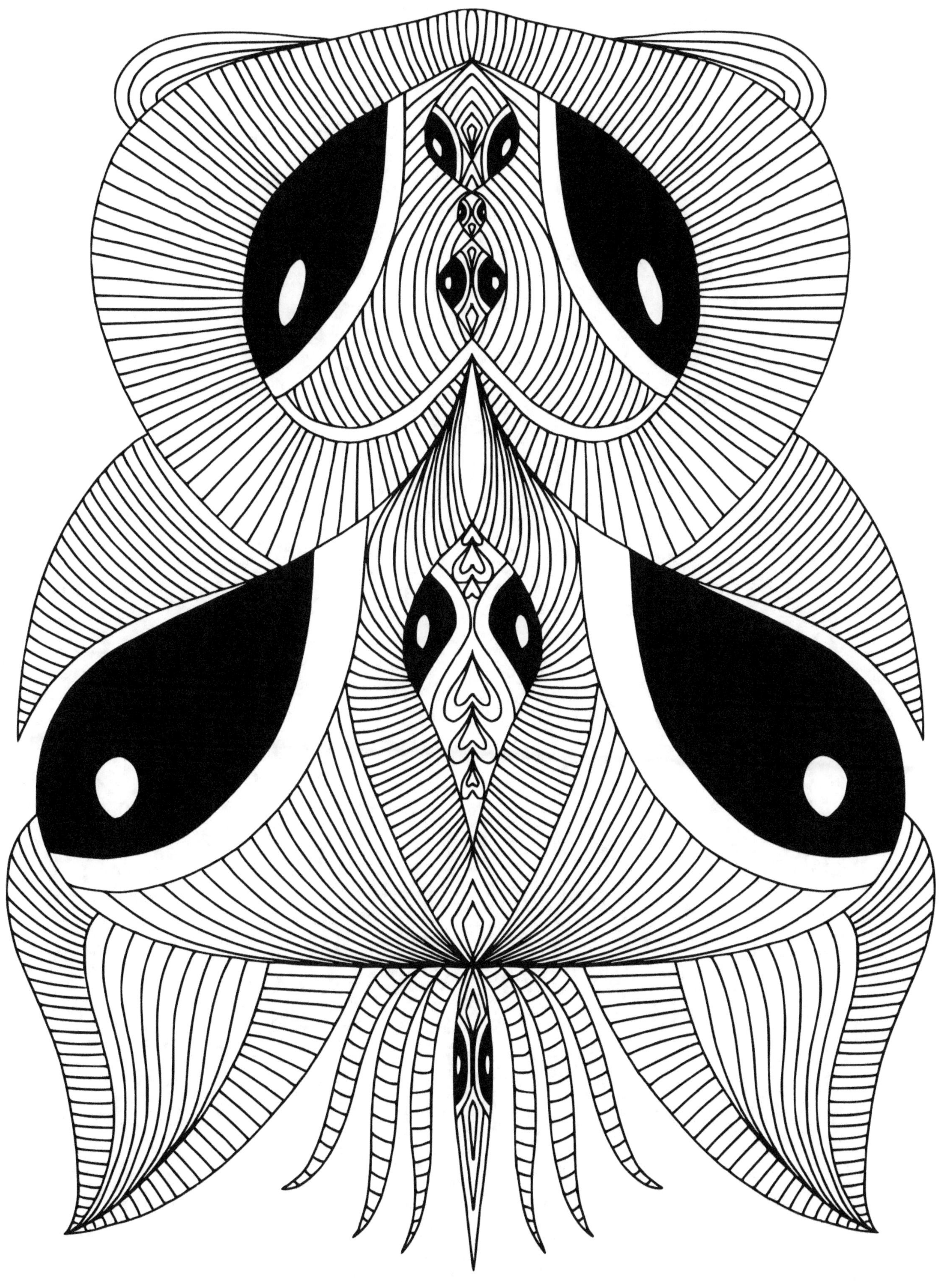

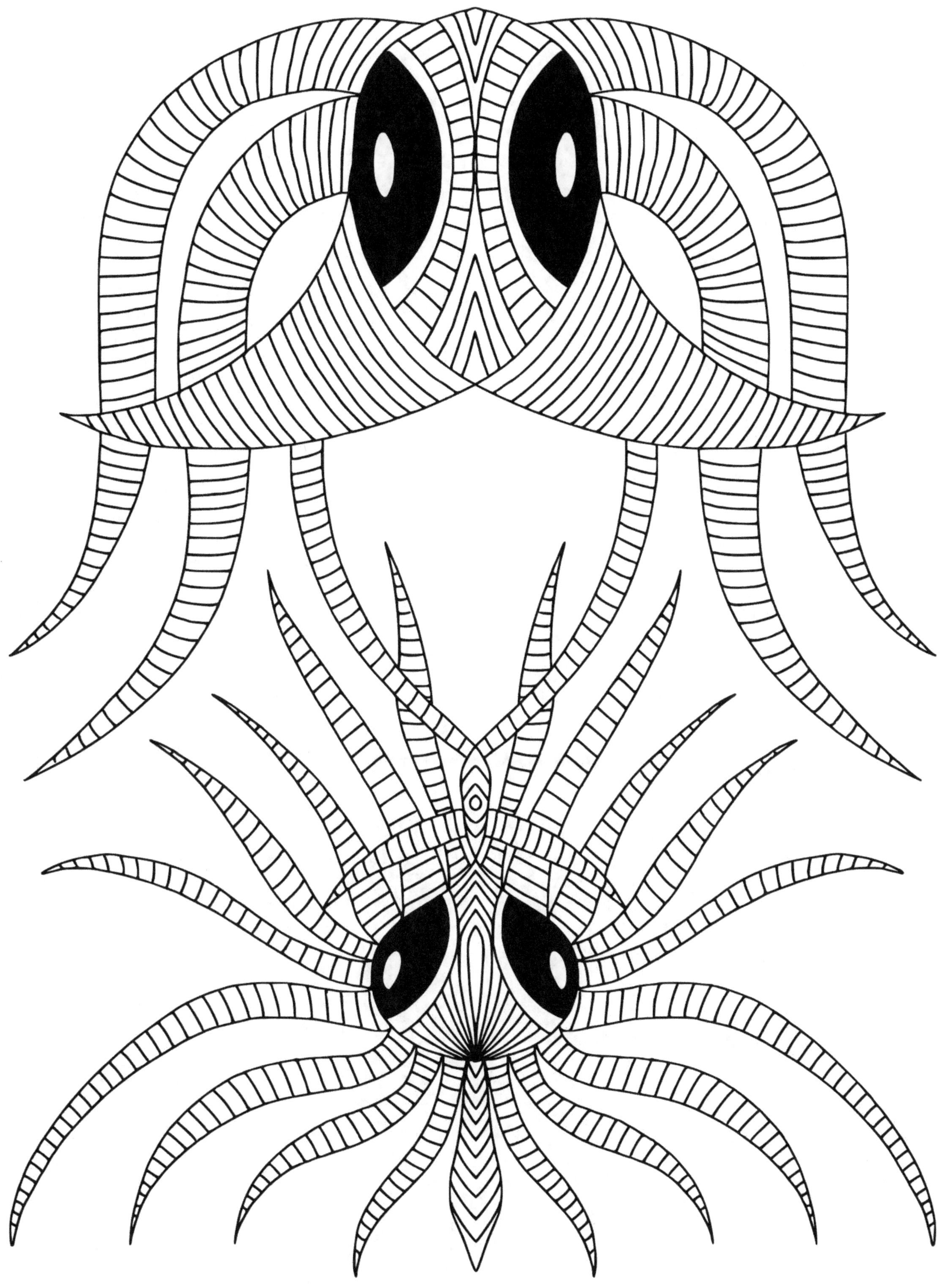

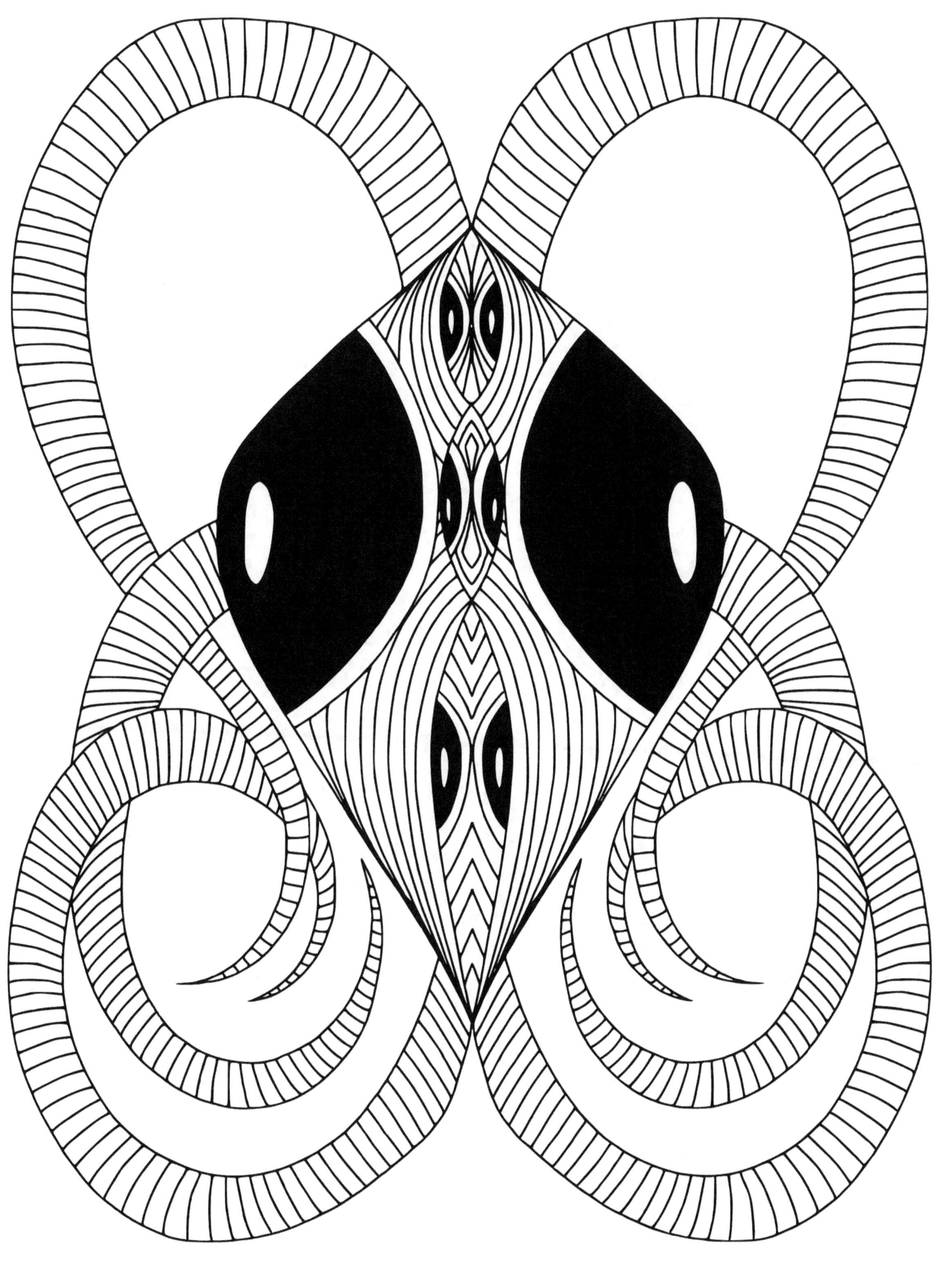

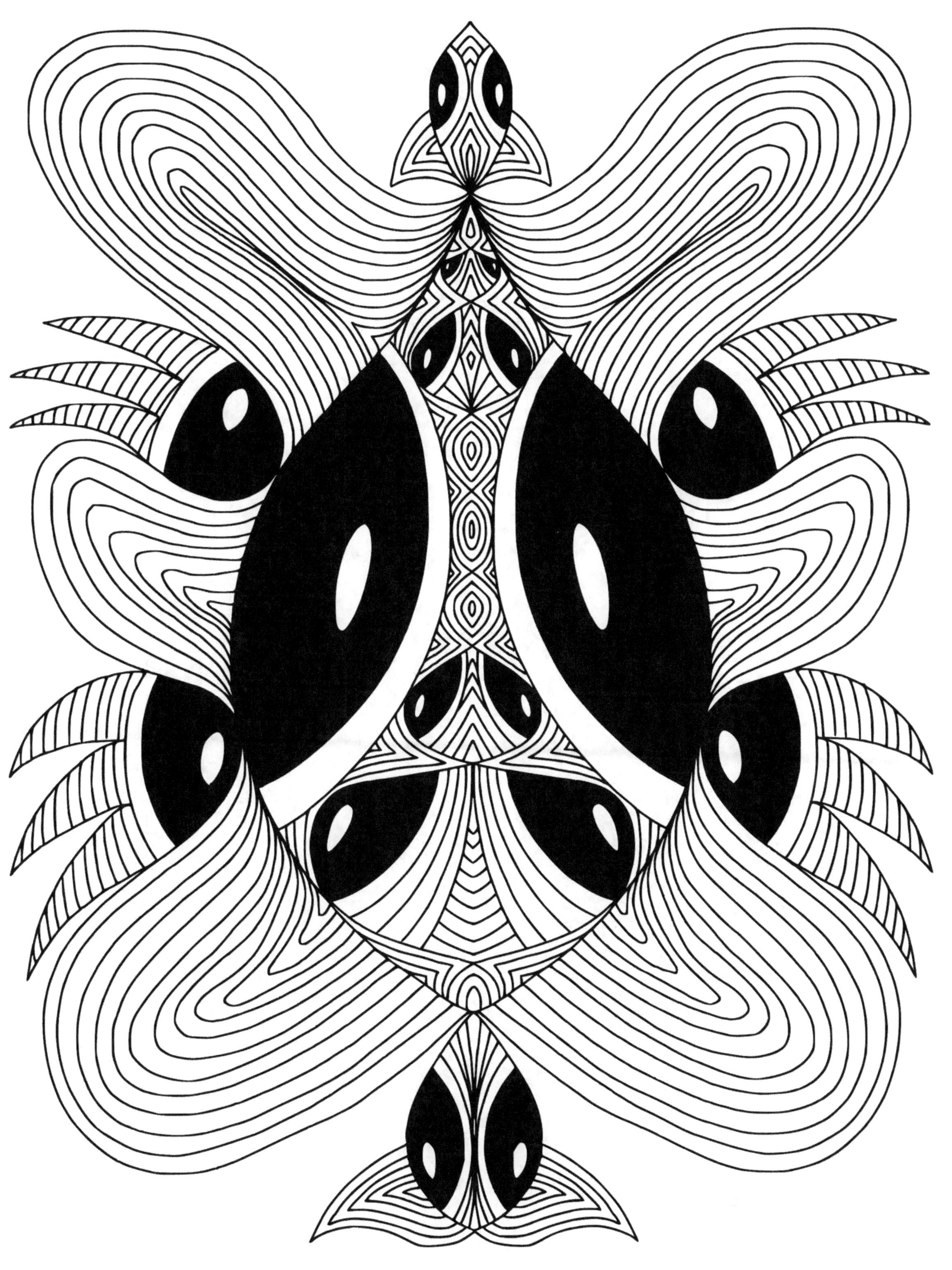

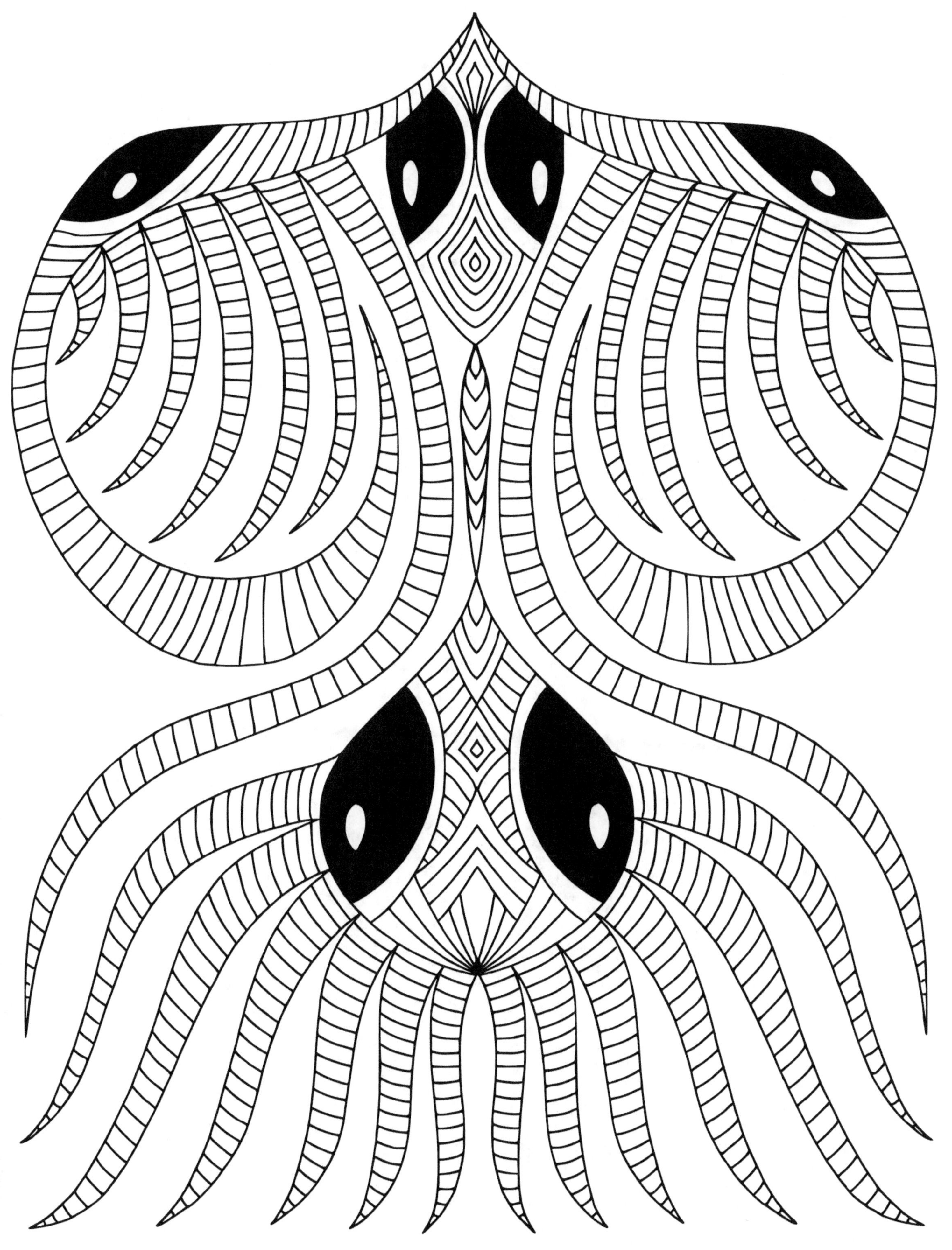

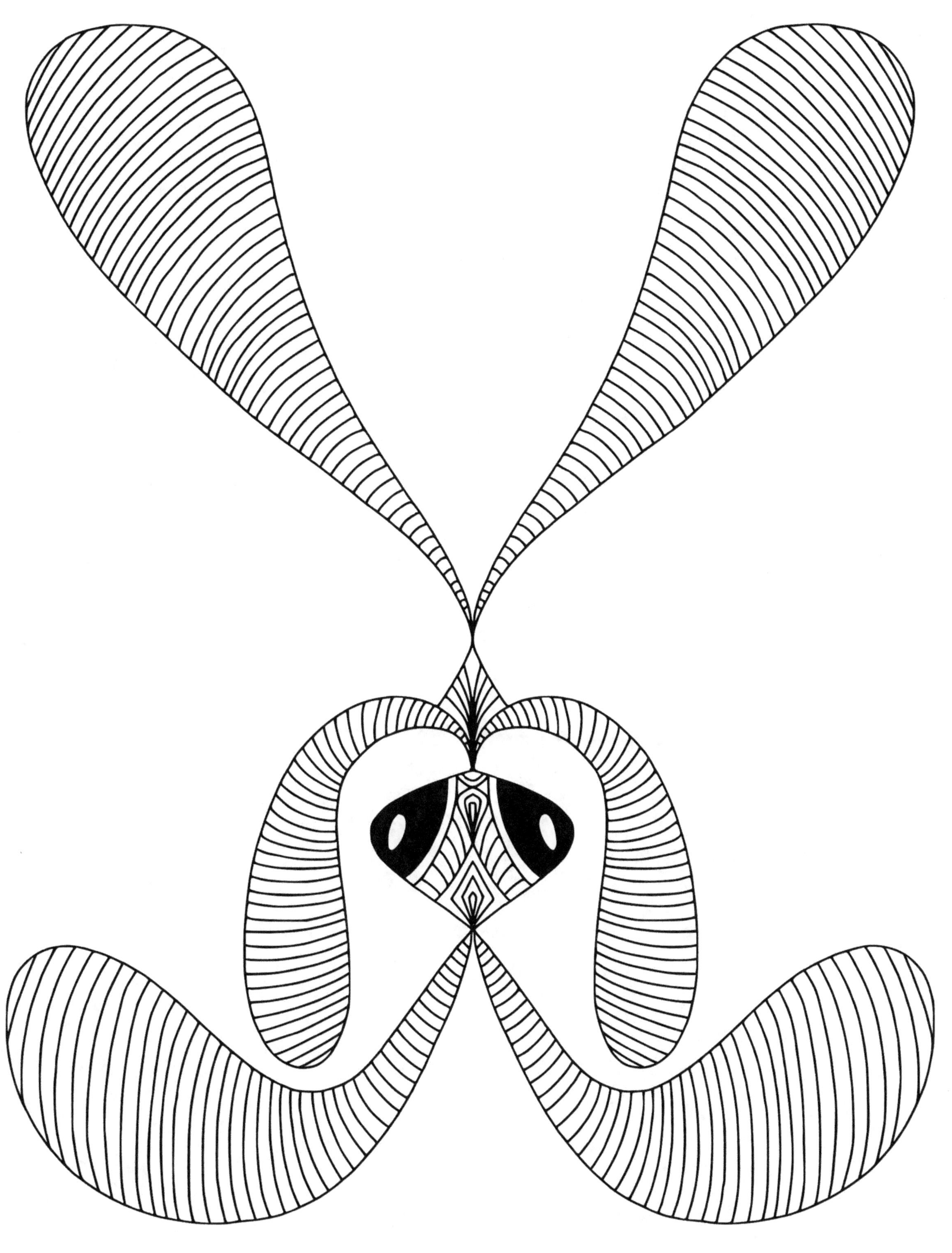

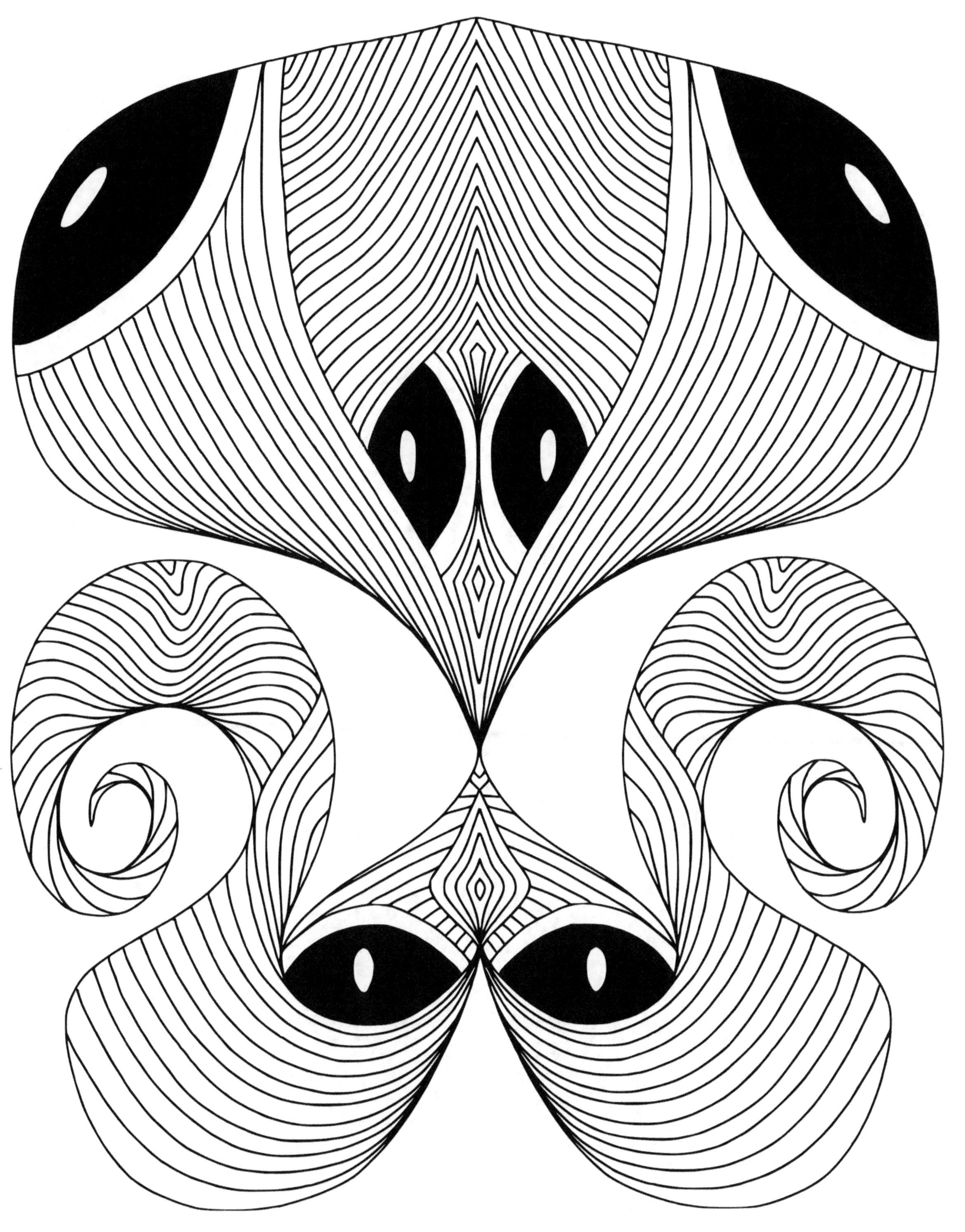

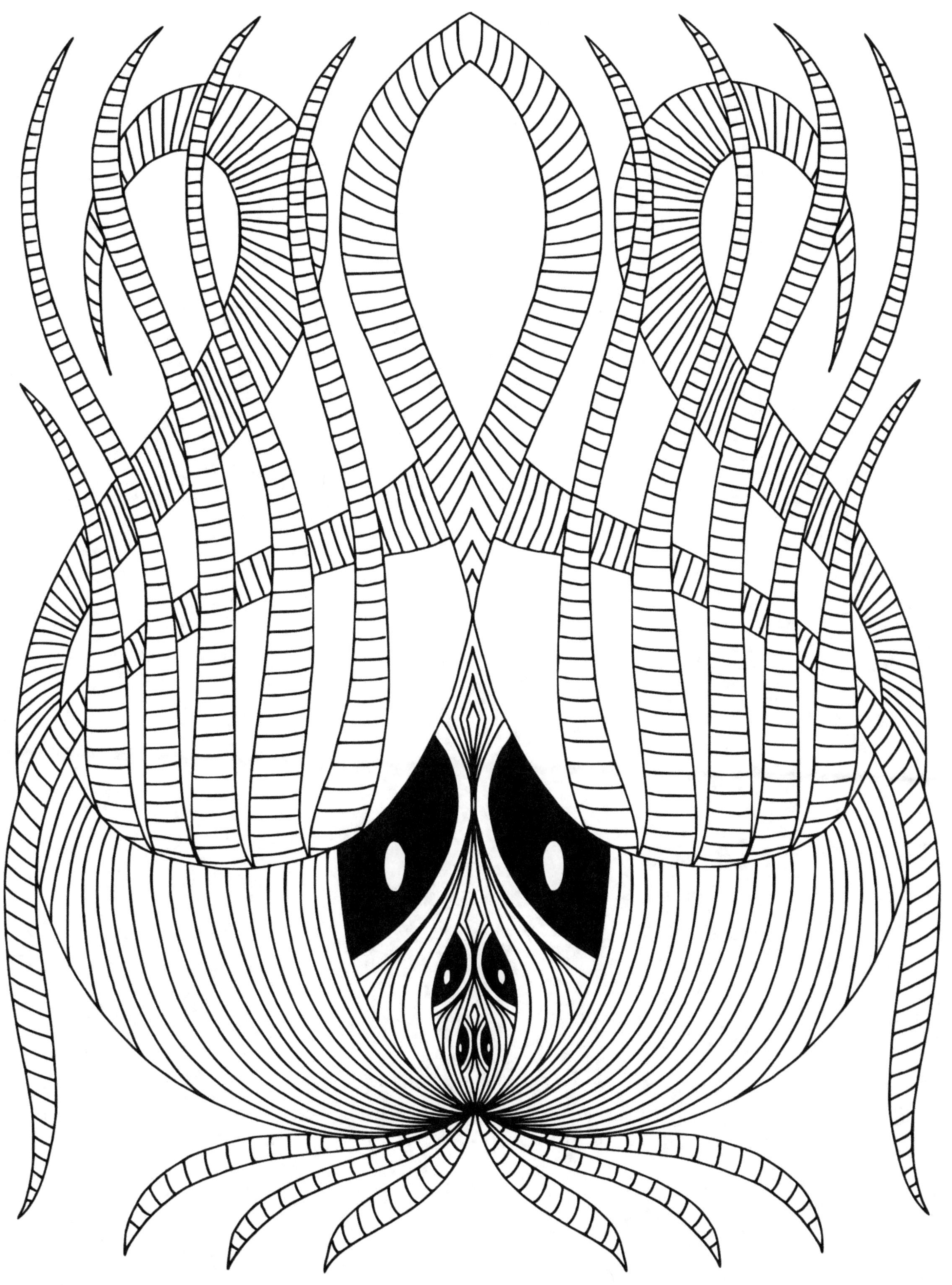

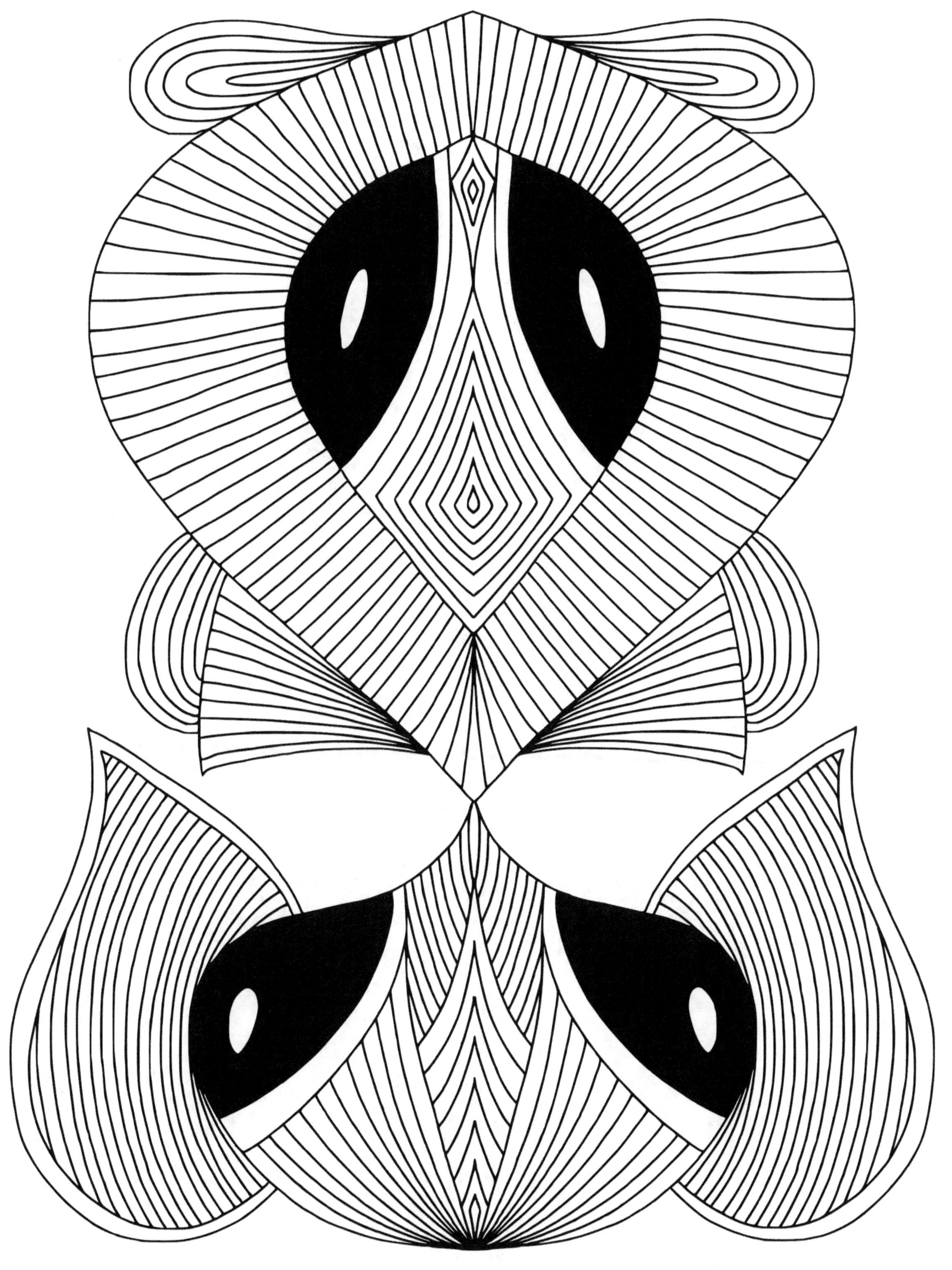

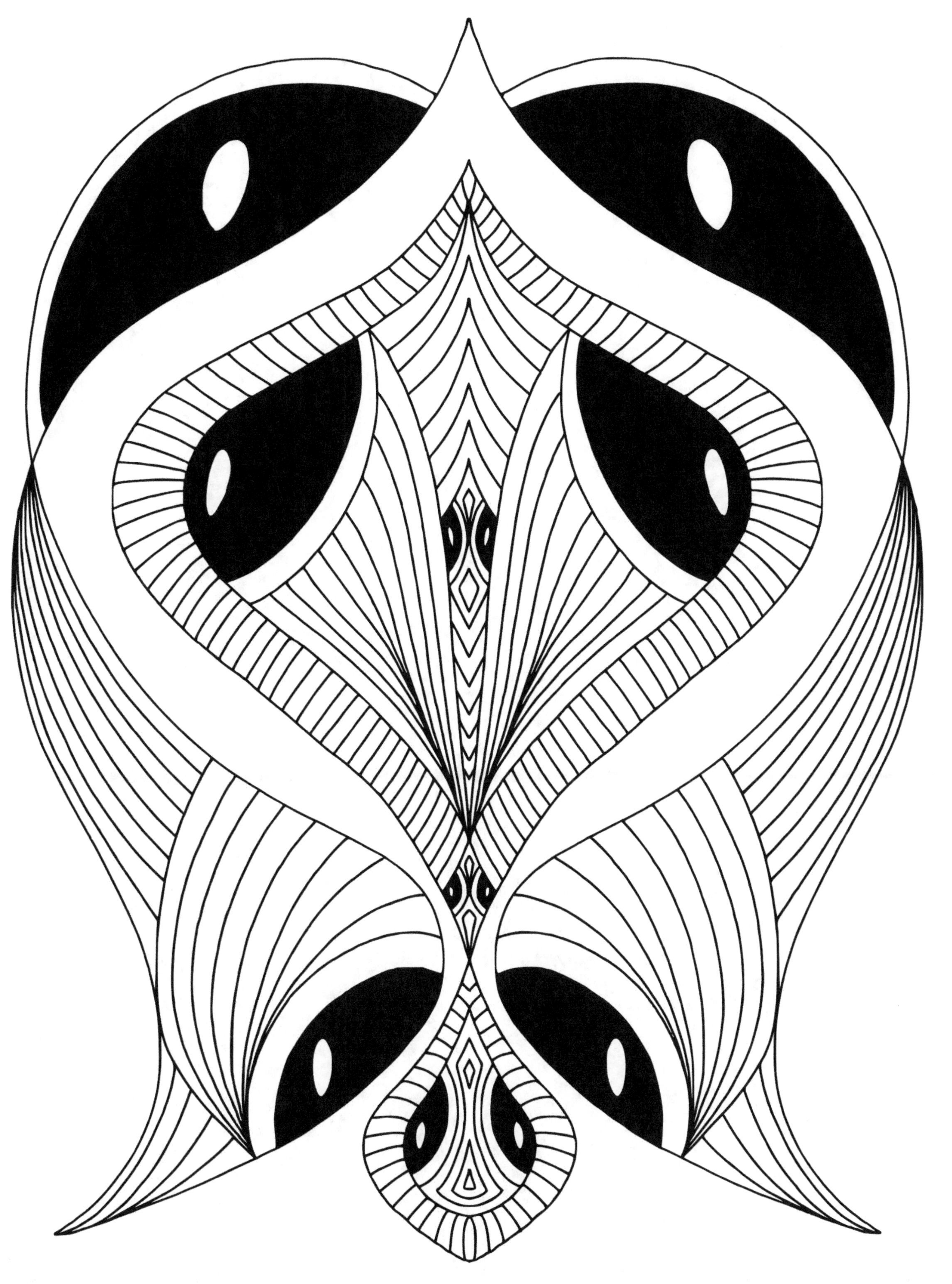

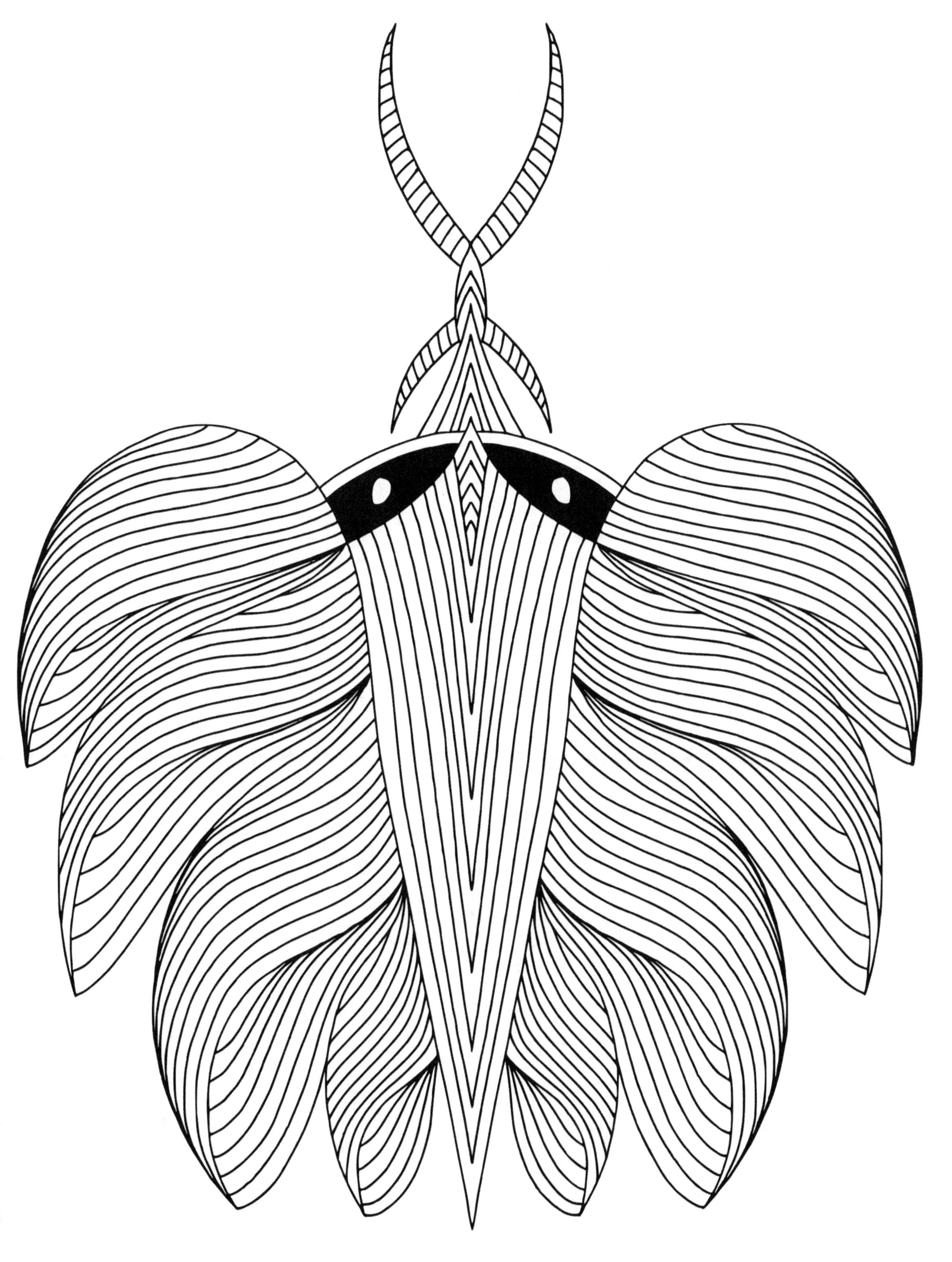

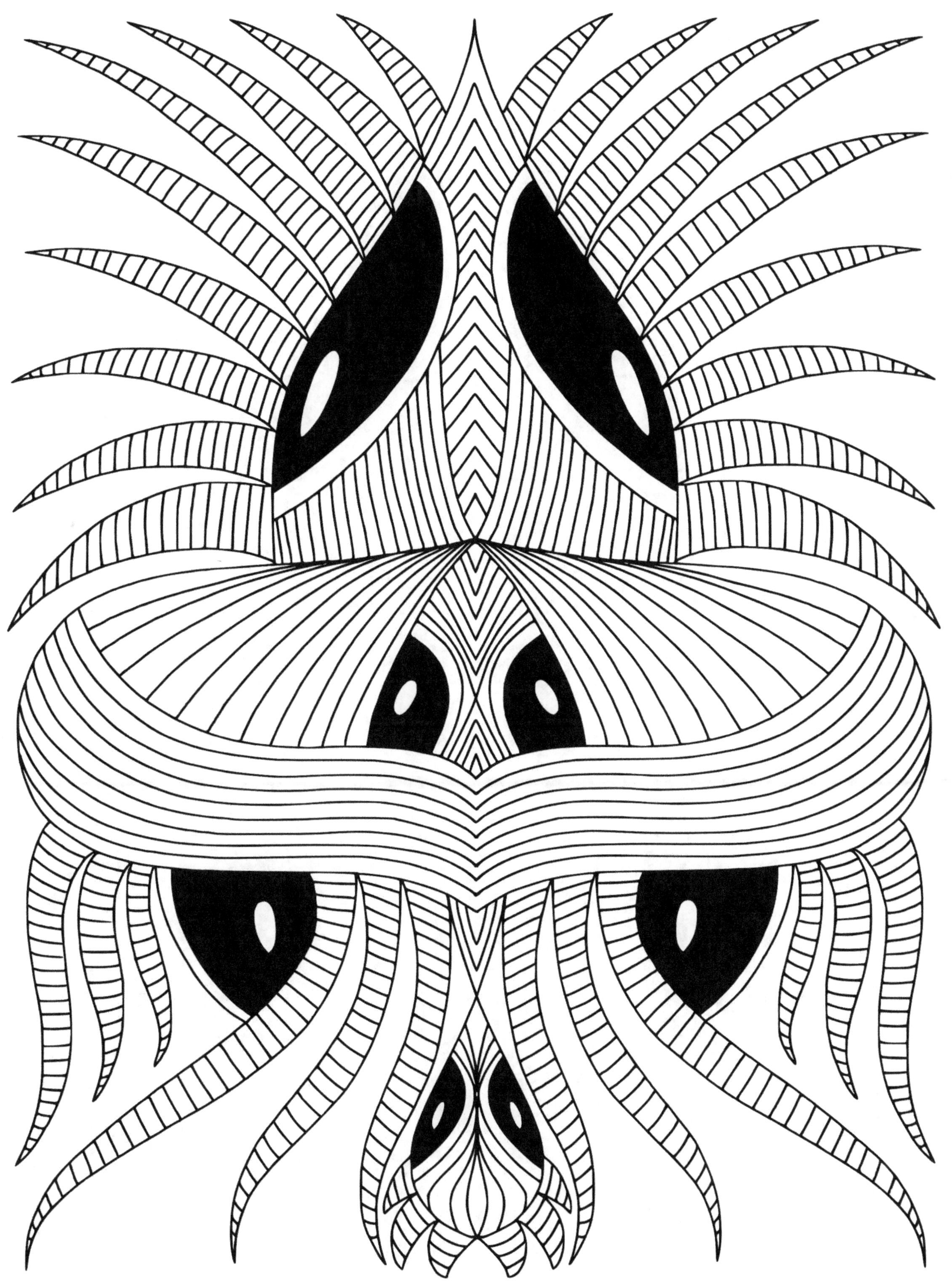

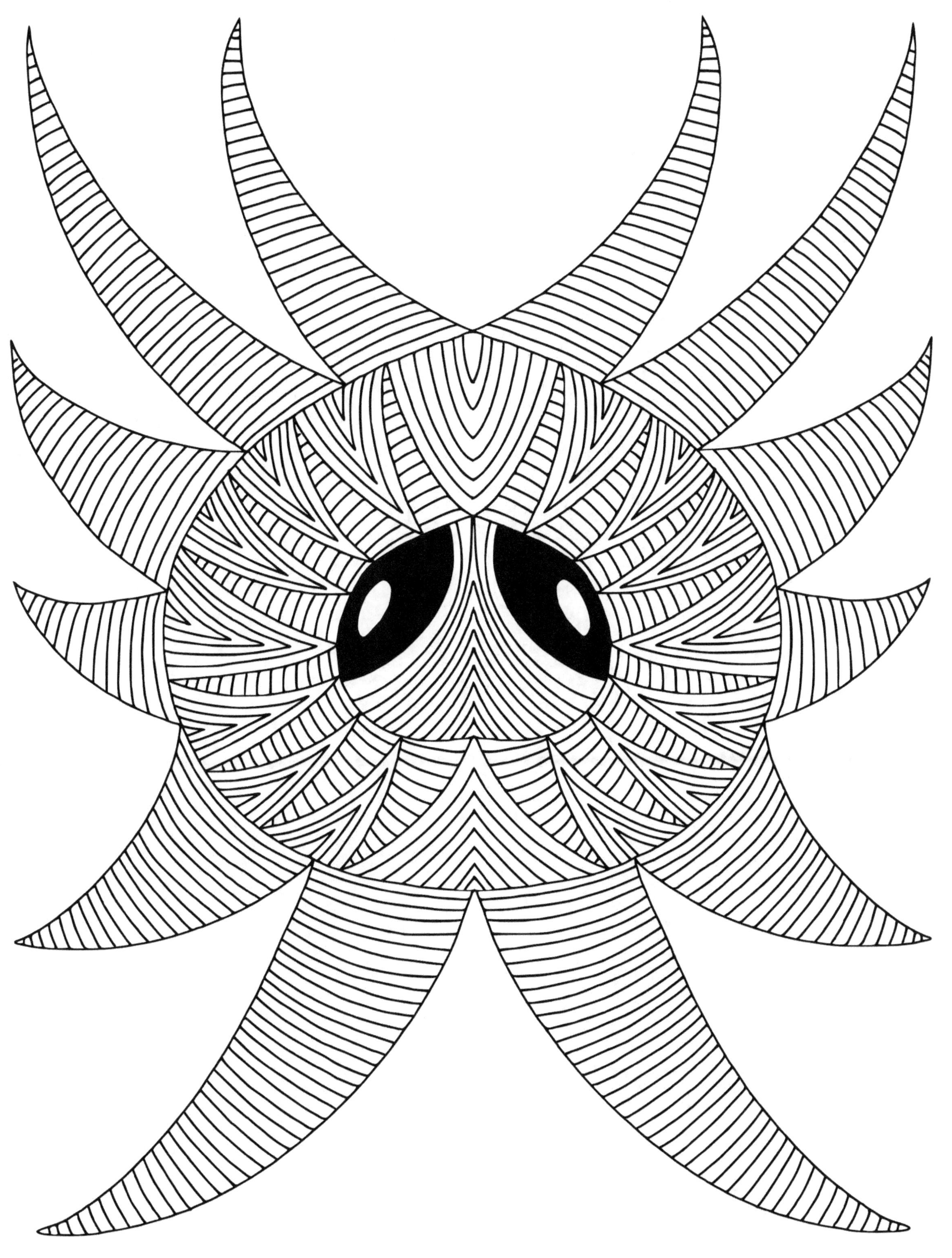

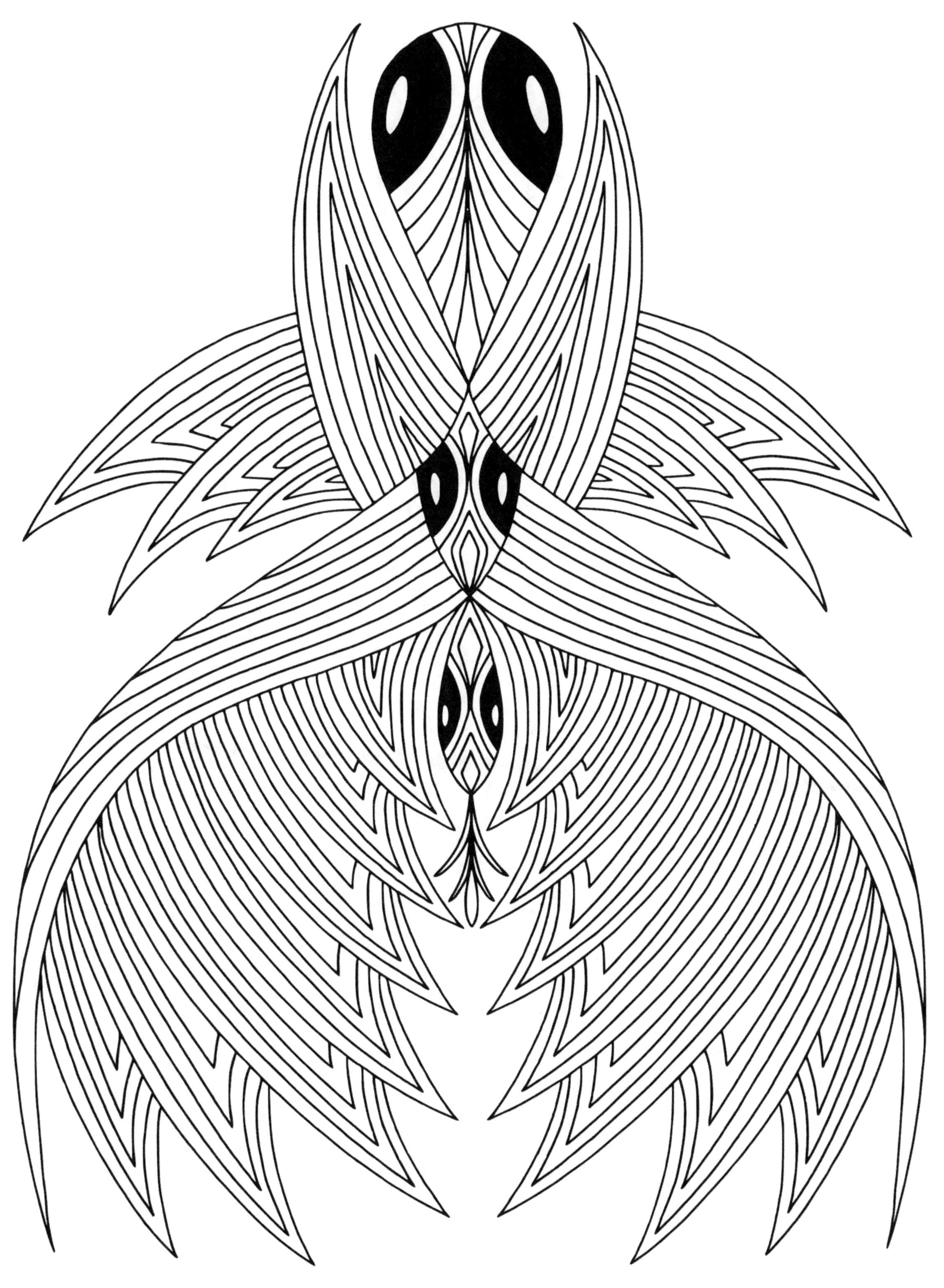

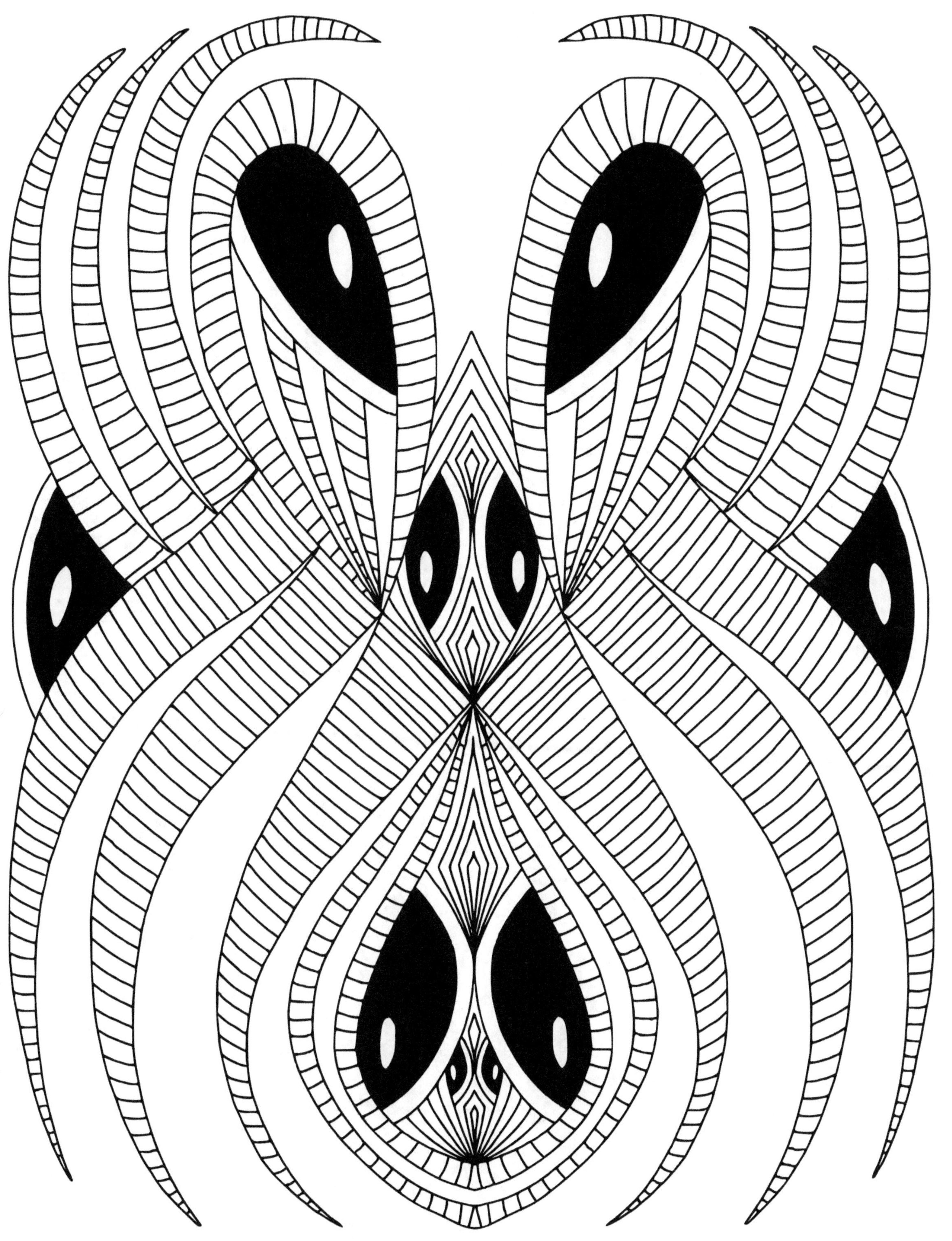

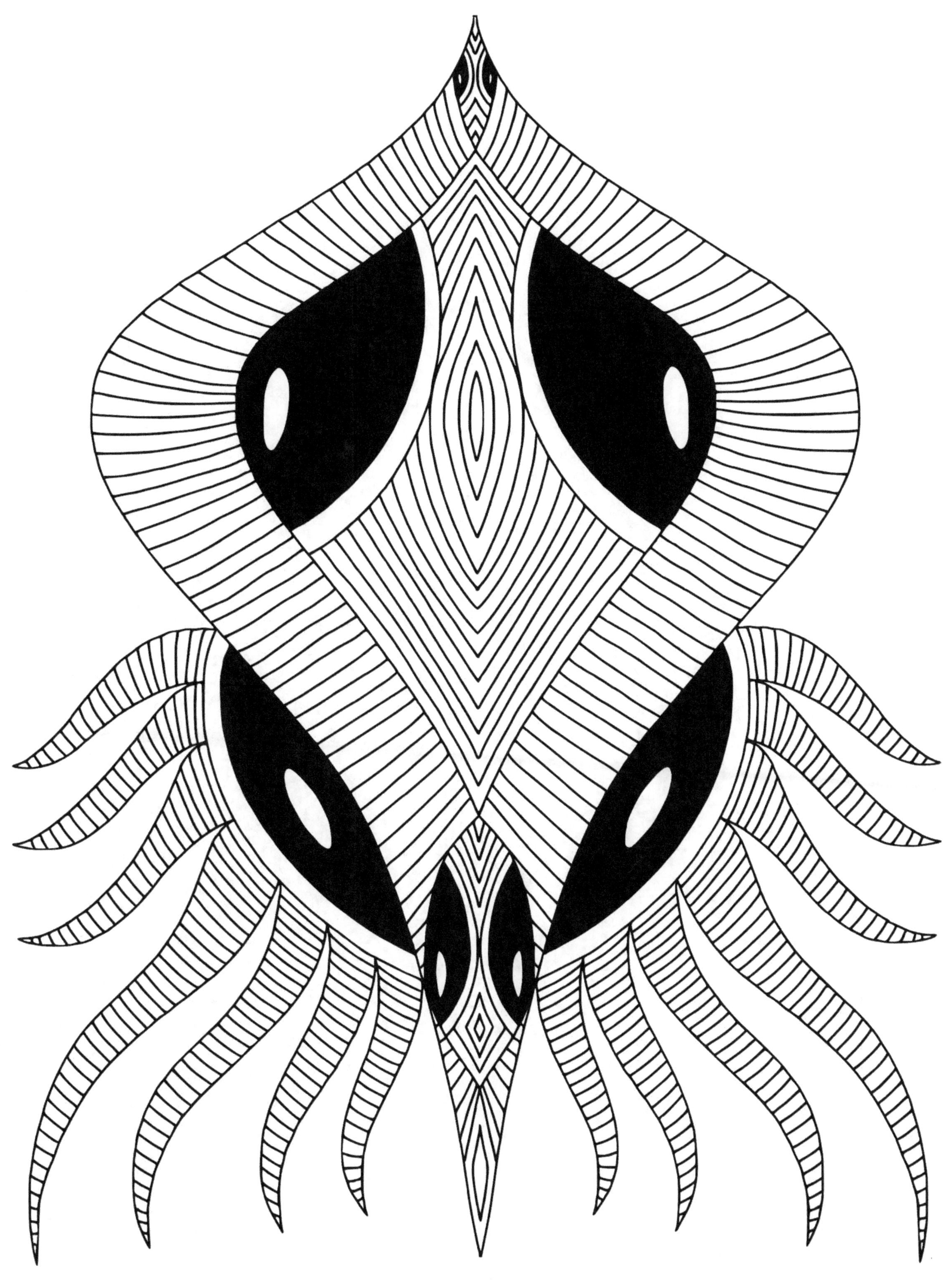

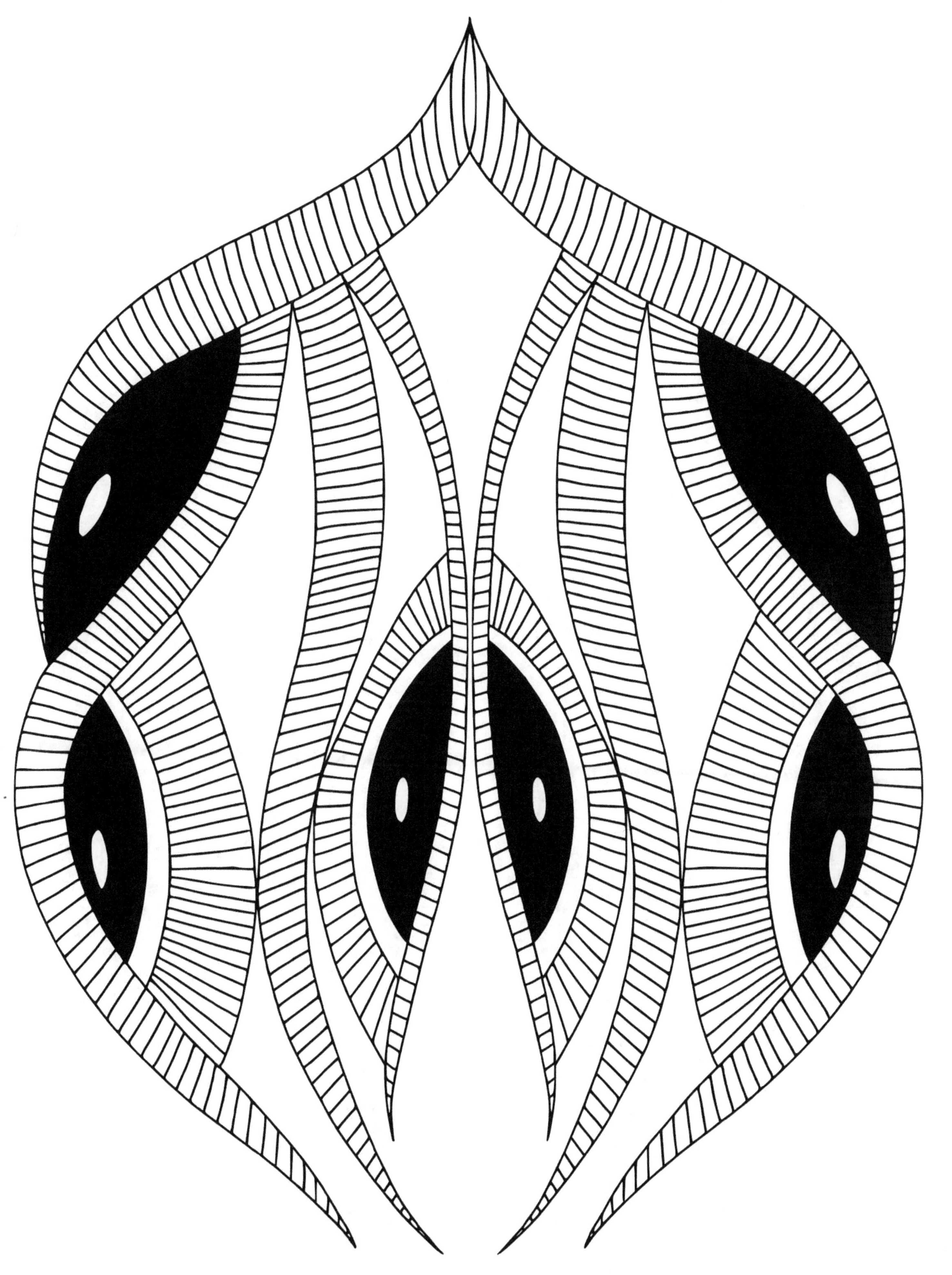

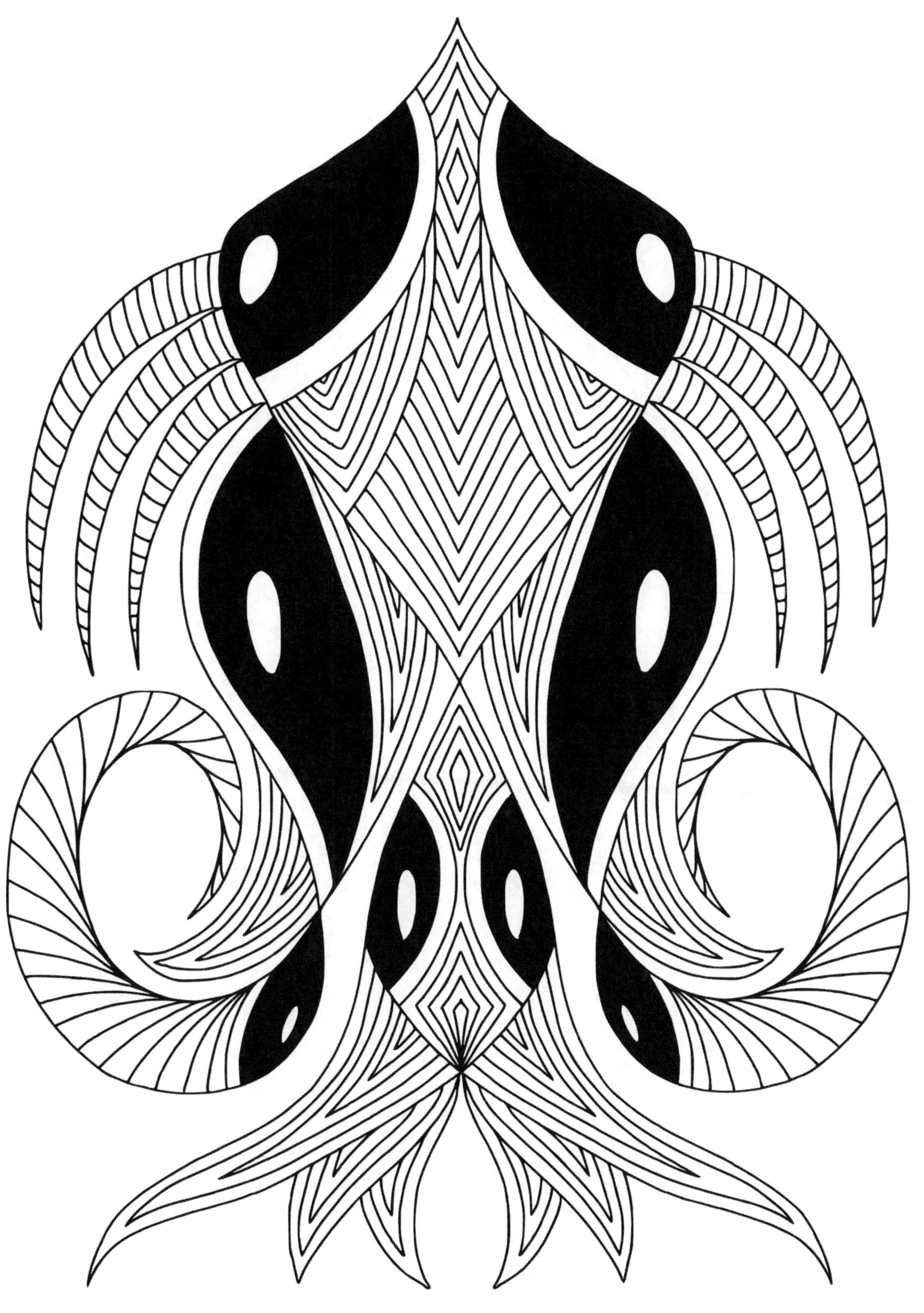

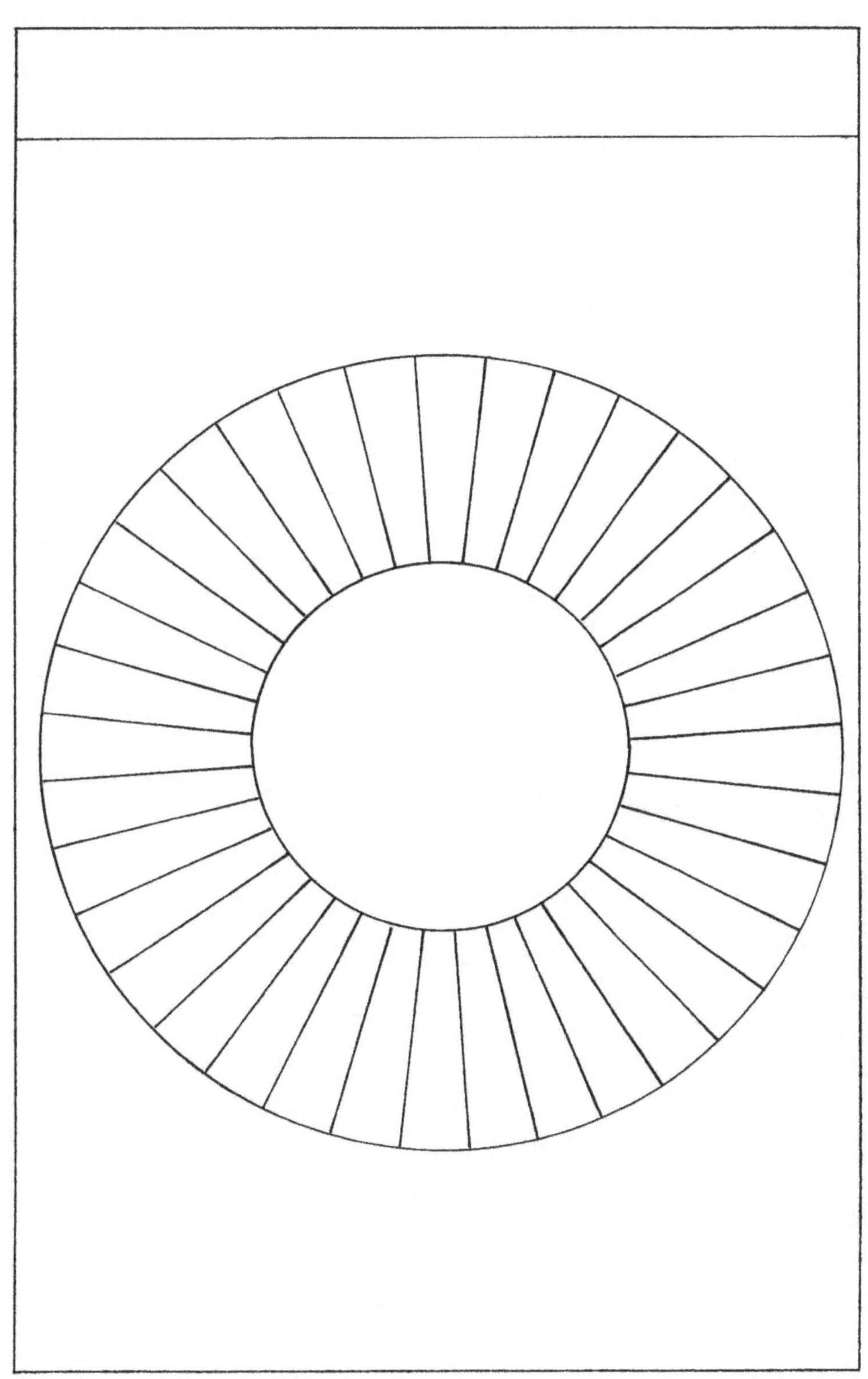

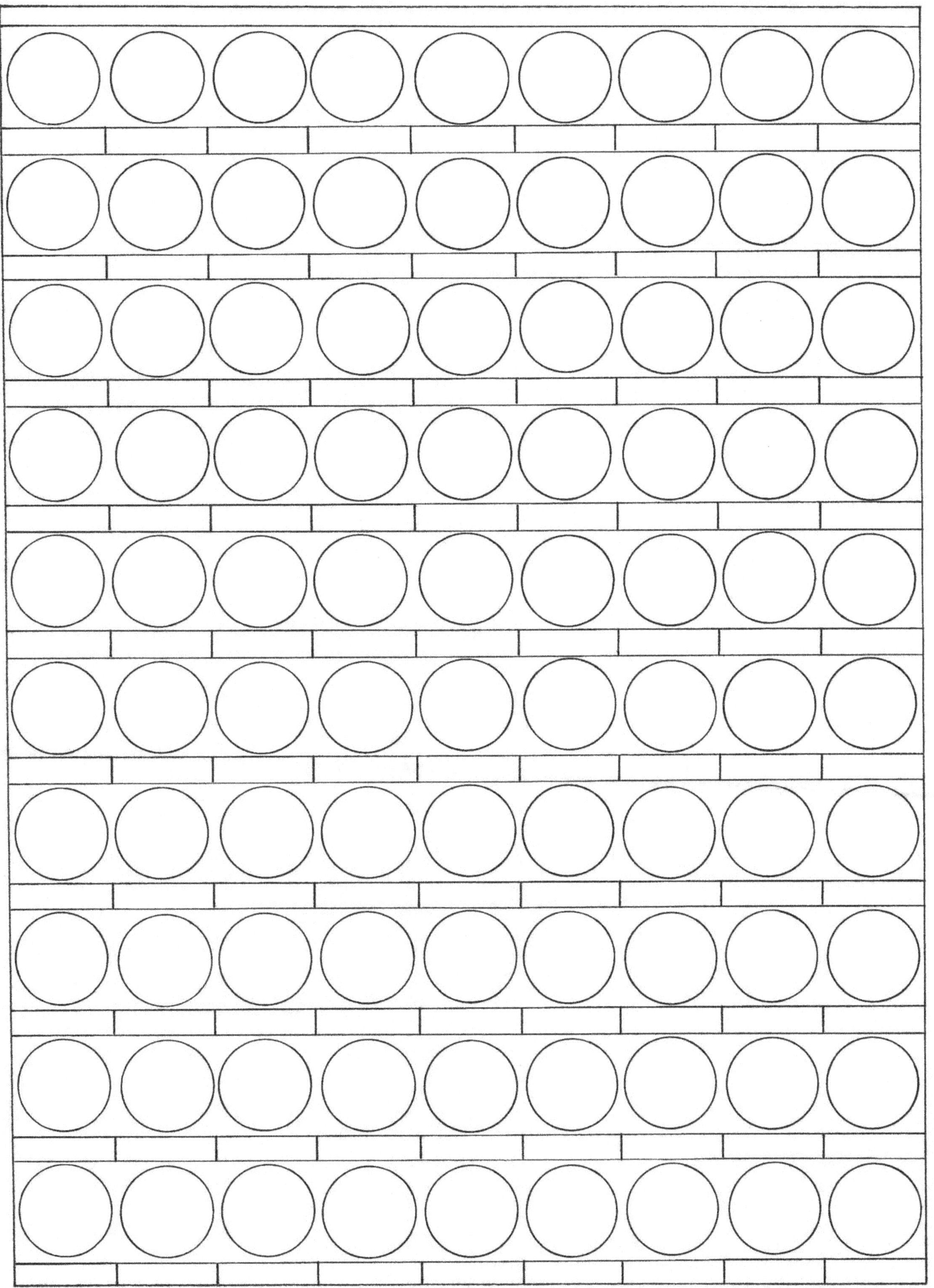